Robert Jones works at Wolff Olins, the London and New York consulting firm, where he advises chief executives of national and global corporations on how to create and manage their big idea.

He's fascinated by the emotional side of business – the way that most business people are driven by something much more complex than merely the desire to make money.

The spirit of the new economy, he believes, goes much deeper than the internet and e-business. It's a new climate, a new mood, which recognizes the power of emotion, which challenges complacent corporations, which destroys old categories, and brings customers and employees together in completely new kinds of community. In a phrase, it's a new and better kind of capitalism – and what we've seen so far is just the beginning.

Robert Jones lives in Highbury, north London.

contents

acknowledgements

I want at the outset to thank all the people who've made this book possible.

The book is based on interviews with leaders in a wide range of organizations with big ideas. I'm very grateful to all of these leaders: Andrew Armishaw, Nancy Brown Johnson, Sir John Browne, Barbara Cassani, Martin Drury, Eduoard Ettegui, Jane Frost, Rob Furness, Akira Gemma, Rajat Gupta, Sir Stuart Hampson, Patrick Holden, Michael Jackson, Ingvar Kamprad, Ariga Kaoru, Bruce Kemp, Anders Knutsen, Brian Larcombe, Terry Leahy, Julian Metcalfe, Sir Mark Moody-Stuart, Deepak Parekh, Peter Pearce, Alan Rusbridger, Andrew Smith, Hans Snook, Ratan Tata, Alun Thomas and Thomas Wellauer.

Many people have pointed me in new directions, or helped in practical ways. First – in all sorts of ways – my parents. But also Beat Amstutz, Hans Arnold, Julie Baddeley, Peter Barrett, Alex Cameron, Elly Crichton Stuart, Jonathan Day, John Diefenbach, Jesús Encinar, Bob Garratt, Shari Grossman, Doug Hamilton, Pam Hurley, Pam T. Job, Jens Jungen, Jonathan Knowles, Sir Stuart Lipton, Kate Manasian, Wally Olins, Liz Padmore, Grace Palmer, Stewart Palmer, Chris Rowan, Jane Scruton, Robin Sibley, Paula Snyder, Beth Stimpson, Rupert Stubbs, Luke Swanson, Martin Trees, Michael Wallis, Jane Wentworth, John Williamson, Harry White and Michael Zur-Szpiro.

My first two research assistants played a huge role in getting the book off the ground: Sean McKnight and Veronika Tarasowa.

Over the six months in which most of the research, and all of the writing, has been done, one person has been invaluable and indispensable, as researcher, reviewer and mission control: Carmen Miranda.

Andrew Lownie has been the ideal agent: enthusiast, advocate and friend. Lucinda McNeile and Sarah Hodgson at HarperCollins have been immensely determined, enthusiastic and deft editors.

Mani Norland designed the cover, and James Tye took my photograph.

Val Allam and Jules Lubbock have both been extremely generous with their time in reading drafts of the book and discussing with me their reactions. During our conversations, Jules made many quietly profound observations, which I hope I've accurately taken on board.

I'm particularly grateful to Charles Wright, managing director of Wolff Olins, for supporting me in this project, and giving me the time to write the book. Most organizations find it all too easy to say no to new ideas: Wolff Olins is different.

And Brian Boylan, chairman of Wolff Olins and my unofficial mentor over the eight years I've worked here, has influenced – subtly or directly – almost every page of the book. Many of the ideas here have grown out of conversations we've had as we've worked together on projects for clients, and Brian has been a wise, warm and generous source of inspiration.

Most important of all, Neil McKenna, my partner, has done more than anyone to make this book happen. He got excited about the book's potential before I did, encouraged me to turn the original thought into a proposal, reacted almost instantly to my drafts as I wrote them, and helped me draw much bigger thoughts out of my initial notions. No one could have been more devoted in guiding the project across the shadow between conception and creation, between the initial impulse and the printed book. Thank you.

hello, in twelve languages

Visit the London headquarters of Orange, and the first thing you see is a banner over reception saying 'hello' in a dozen different languages. The next thing you notice is the sign pointing to the top-floor 'imaginarium' and the office of the 'director of futurology'. You know that something special is going on here.

Orange is one of the world's most remarkable communication companies. Five years ago, it didn't exist. Now, it's the best-performing British mobile phone network, and there are Orange networks in a dozen other countries, from Holland to Hong Kong. Most significantly of all, in a fickle marketplace, Orange has the most loyal of customers: its 'churn rate' – the number of customers who defect each year – is significantly lower than the industry standard.

What has driven all this?

Not its technical performance, or its customer service, or its pricing. Coverage and call quality are good, but you can wait hours to get through to Orange's call centre; and other networks are cheaper.

Nor is it Orange's business model – that's changing. Originally Orange thought it was in the 'wire-free' business, but now it's evolving into a much broader kind of communication company, offering services people reach from their highly wired-up PCs.

What drives Orange is the conviction with which it was

set up. The two hundred people who created Orange shared a view, not about what technology could do, but about what it *ought to do* for people. They didn't see why mobile phones should be bulky or hard to use. They rejected the first phone Nokia developed for them – it was just too big. They didn't see why people should be forced to pay for itemized billing. They knew that market research wouldn't tell them what services to provide – as they say, you can't research the future. But they could see (sometimes faintly) a million new things people would be able to do, once mobile phones were ubiquitous. And they could see that Orange would be there, providing all those things.

It's very hard to put this view into words. They've tried. They have a mission statement, a philosophy statement, and no fewer than three different lists of values. But these are all just words. Recently, they've started using a phrase, 'a bright human future', but some of their people feel uneasy about it: the very word 'human' sounds inhuman, sounds like science fiction.

Some people at Orange talk about an image that sums up their conviction: it's a photograph of a seven-year-old child leading an adult by the hand. It's about a kind of childlike (but not childish) simplicity, it's about the days when you couldn't wait for the future, rather than fearing its arrival.

Probably the best summary of the idea is a phrase from the launch advertising campaign: 'the future's bright, the future's Orange'. It's about optimism. Equally, it's about the company's level of energy and size of ambition.

What's remarkable is the way that this conviction is shared by people outside and inside the company. Orange talks about 'Orange people': a community which includes both customers and employees. Customers feel like more than customers: they belong to something.

When Orange was being set up one of the company's innovations was that it would interact with its customers, not just (like other phone companies) serve them. Its customer magazine is one of the liveliest around. And its main way of researching new product ideas is still to test them on customers – it launches them and measures take-up. Customers therefore contribute to and help shape Orange.

Orange is driven by an idea – something hard to pin down, but emotional, and widely shared. A big idea.

The same is true of IKEA. It too has a sense of purpose that goes beyond its own profit, a sense of purpose that has captured the imaginations of both its customers and its employees. Of course, IKEA needs to make a profit. Of course, people work there because they need to make a living. And of course, people buy IKEA products because they're mostly well made and often astonishingly cheap. But those economic considerations are only one aspect of IKEA. People don't just buy IKEA, they buy into it – into an idea that mingles style, thrift, self-help, plainness, Scandinavia, classlessness and all sorts of other things. They choose IKEA not through economic logic, but through what you might call 'emotional logic'. Ask IKEA's founder, Ingvar Kamprad, for the secret of the company's success, and his answer is simple: 'We are a concept company.'

The things people buy – products and services – are becoming more and more similar as it becomes increasingly easy for one company to copy another's technological advantage. This has a simple but devastating consequence:

in the absence of economic differences, emotional logic will become the single most important business driver.

The *consumers* of the future will expect and demand choice, but that choice will be more between different emotional worlds than between different product features.

The *employees* of the future will be more independent-minded and more mobile, readier to change job or career or even continent. They will join, and help shape, organizations that reflect their own values.

The *investors* of the future will be less obsessed with short-term 'shareholder value'. Intangibles will matter more, and organizations will be assessed on their social and environmental contribution.

In some ways, business has always been about emotional logic, has always answered deeper human needs than merely profit. The Swedish word for business, *näringslivet*, means 'nourishment for life'. Tomorrow's successful companies will be those that nourish life best.

How to nourish life

Big ideas can be about all sorts of things. But, in order to nourish life, they all have two dimensions in common.

First, they are much more than just rational, logical, cerebral. They have depth. They create a special and palpable spirit in the business. They make an encounter with the organization into a distinctive experience.

Second, they appeal equally to people inside and outside the organization: they're a social property, belonging to everyone and no one. They dissolve the boundaries between customers, employees, suppliers, outsourcers, investors and so on so that all these people become members of the same thing.

IKEA has such a big idea. But you don't have to own hundreds of near-identical superstores to have one.

Mandarin Oriental owns a handful of rather special hotels in Hong Kong, Bangkok, San Francisco and elsewhere, each with its own feel and identity. Yet the hotels are united by a big idea that's about *moments of pleasure* – an experience that's special but not exclusive, luxurious but not extravagant, oriental yet approachable. The idea is shared by Mandarin Oriental's staff and its wide circle of committed clients.

Orange has a big idea. But you don't have to be a consumer business to have one.

The management consultants McKinsey have an aura that's unique in their field. Their big idea is about 'rigour'. It's about the very brightest people advising clients at the highest level, with the ethos (and the fees) of a law firm. And this aura is just as palpable to clients as to McKinsey's own people.

Nor, finally, do you have to be a commercial organization to have a big idea.

The National Trust, Britain's most distinguished conservation charity, preserves places of historic interest or natural beauty for everyone to enjoy. Its big idea, 'places for people for ever', inspires not only its staff but also a huge body of ordinary people who've become members – well over two million of them.

But why does a big idea matter? What's going on in the world that makes big ideas suddenly so important? Or are they just a passing fad?

How do you find one, communicate it and manage it?

Is a big idea just another management tool, or is it more organic than that? If you don't have one, can you acquire one? And if you do, can you lose it?

How, in short, do you make an organization that nourishes life? That's the story this book sets out to tell.

CHAPTER ONE

what's next?

On the outskirts of a northern industrial city in Britain stands a huge, grey high-tech shed. It looks like a large hypermarket or a small airport terminal. But there's no name on it: it's anonymous and slightly forbidding. Around the site there's a tall fence. Drive up to security and there's no human being on duty: instead you press a button, speak through an intercom, and someone unseen lets you in.

Inside the shed there's a different world. It's a vast space, populated by a thousand or more people working at desks, most of them busy on the phone. It's all people. There's no cash, no vaults, no cheques even, yet this is a bank.

This is First Direct, the world's pioneer in telephone banking.

First Direct matters. It's a small bank, with around a million customers, but it's emblematic of a much larger social shift. Behind First Direct, there's a compelling story, and an even more explosive question.

The compelling story is about what the bank has achieved.

Ten years ago, First Direct brought the idea of customer service into banking. In a world of marble halls, faceless staff and inflexible procedures, First Direct had a simple, but at the time revolutionary, idea: banking to suit the customer. A bank that was open 24 hours a day, 365 days a year. A bank that, if it made a mistake, would sort things out quickly and even compensate you, without your having to ask. A bank that, because it had no branches, was much cheaper to run. A bank that wouldn't charge you for running your account. And above all a bank that saw that the heart of banking isn't cheque-processing or bullion-handling or loan-approving: it's managing relationships with customers.

But now First Direct faces an explosive question. Its customers have got used to excellent customer service. They want something more. The question in the air at First Direct, literally, is 'what's next?' Literally, because this is the headline of the bank's current advertising campaign, displayed on posters hung from the ceiling around the giant shed. But metaphorically, it's also the main business question the bank must face.

The frenzy of possibility

It's a question that sooner or later every other organization will have to confront. Once you've achieved high quality in your products, or excellent standards in your customer service, where do you go? What's next? And it's more than just a question: it's a whole climate. It's the predominant mood at the start of the new century. We live in a world not of answers but of questions. There's an endemic impatience with the status quo, a feverish pursuit of the next big thing.

Indeed, there's a kind of delight in the fever. In a strange way, we don't want answers. The pleasure is in the chase. The fun is in travelling, not arriving. We want the possibilities to stay open. It's perhaps a natural enough feeling at the start of a century. We feel that the new century must feel significantly different from the old one, but it's too early to decide *how* it should be different.

The fever is nowhere more evident than in the world of business.

There's an obsession with hunting down the next great way to make money, the next thing that's really exciting. And what gets people excited is the hunt itself: as soon as a new idea has been found, it's no longer so new, no longer 'next'.

There's never been so much emotion in business. 'What will happen', says Sir John Browne of BP, 'is based on emotional drives. That's why you can't predict the future. If people worked on pure economic logic, I could predict the future, but I can't.'

The terms in which the fever is discussed change by the month. Not long ago, the smart phrase was 'fast companies'. Then it was 'the new economy'. In a few weeks, the buzz will have moved on again. Meanwhile, every week brings news of another giant merger, or another innovative demerger. The fun is not in settling things but in unsettling them.

But it's not just commercial companies that are caught up in this. Public agencies are finding completely different ways to deliver services, by phone or internet. Suddenly, government no longer needs to feel like bureaucracy. Non-governmental organizations like Greenpeace now find themselves among the most powerful bodies in the world, courted by governments and multinationals. Suddenly, interest groups no longer feel like militant outsiders.

In this climate of huge possibility, organizations feel free to do almost anything. Supermarkets sell cars. Newsagents become internet service providers. Oil companies campaign for human rights. Charities offer credit cards. There's a universal impulse – like nothing we've ever seen before – to leap over old boundaries.

And people no longer fit into compartments. It's increasingly hard to categorize people by their social background, their job or their age. More importantly, we don't *want* to be categorized. Stereotypes – such as 'the *Guardian* reader' in Britain – no longer make sense. This was the wispy-bearded, muesli-eating man who drove a 2CV, worked in the public sector and read the *Guardian* newspaper every day. 'There's no longer such a person,' says the paper's current editor, Alan Rusbridger. 'Those were old boxes. People don't live in them any more.'

The desire everywhere is for the future to be radically different from the past. The wish is to keep things open – not to close down possibilities.

As a result, a great shibboleth of twentieth-century business thinking is coming under question. The whole idea of *strategy* is starting to feel wrong. How can you have a five-year strategy – a path mapped out into the future – when the overwhelming mood is to leave every possibility open? Why think of managing as a kind of military campaign – a world of generals and their strategies – when managing has become more like a game?

This mood – this universal 'what's next?' – is the atmosphere in which every organization must now try to flourish. It's not just a world that happens to be full of change and uncertainty: it's a world that *loves* change and uncertainty.

It's a world of frenzy, and therefore of energy. It's a world that's uncertain, and therefore exciting. It's a world that's driven by the future much more than by the past, and it's therefore in the main optimistic.

In this climate, organizations need an idea. They need something that expands the minds of their customers and employees, that widens their possibilities, that takes them out of whatever narrow role they currently play. They need an idea that's big.

The blight of sameness

One reason why there's such a demand for difference in the new century is that the twentieth century created so much sameness.

In the second half of the twentieth century, the world became five times more productive. During the same period, global trade increased twenty-fold. By the end of the century, 90 per cent of the world's population had adopted capitalism and market-based institutions as their under-pinning economic system. All this meant more goods and services, more global trade, freer markets – and much more aggressive competition.

In freer markets, more people set up stalls to sell things. This has meant that, almost everywhere in the world, people now have more choice than ever before.

The lowering of trade barriers has smoothed the flow of products and services across national boundaries. And television and the internet have made it much easier for people to know what's available.

In western economies, the growth of choice is explosive. Take telecoms, for example. In most countries, there are now two or three phone companies, and four or five mobile phone networks. Ten years ago, most ordinary people had one, bureaucratic, slow-moving supplier: the state telephone organization. Increasingly, people can choose where to buy gas or electricity. And a typical television viewer, who might have had four channels available ten years ago, now has hundreds.

The average supermarket now stocks 30,000 different things, compared with 7000 ten years ago. That's more than four times as many kinds of fruit, four times as many varieties of pizza, four times as many sorts of fabric conditioner.

We live in a world of choice, of availability, on a scale never before seen.

At the same time, products and services are getting better. Free markets mean competition, and competition drives up standards while lowering prices.

Things, in general, work.

Cars, for instance, are hugely more reliable than they used to be. In the early 1980s, US cars averaged eight defects per vehicle. Now the figure is one. Indeed, the industry-wide average in 1996 was better than that of the best company in 1989. Electronic consumer goods like televisions and hi-fis just carry on working, year after year.

And good customer service is becoming almost commonplace. Airlines are less high-handed. Banks stay open longer and correct mistakes more readily. You can get a phone connected much more quickly. Even welfare services now call benefits claimants 'clients' and try to treat them as such.

In the world's emerging markets, the same picture is visible: more choice, better quality. In a vast market like India, gradually shedding its closed, protectionist attitudes, consumers now find they have the power to choose. Talk to India's most powerful businessman, Ratan Tata, chairman of the vast Tata group, and his message is clear. 'For the first time, consumers have an opportunity to choose. For the first time, companies that don't think about the consumer are being forced to rethink.'

Behind all this is the simple pressure of competition. As *Fortune* magazine has said, 'In today's economy, more than ever, partly because of the huge amount of venture capital available out there, if you don't create a better deal for your customer someone else will.'

Of course, like everything else in business, improvements are patchy. Quality, and pricing, vary astonishingly from market to market. Trains still run late. Taxi drivers are still rude. A lot of television is rubbish. Financial companies still overcharge for bad advice.

But in general, quality is no longer a differentiator. It's the price of market entry.

So, competition has generated better products and services, almost everywhere around the world. But the rose of near-perfection comes with a thorn: sameness.

As products and services become better and better, they also become increasingly similar. If one organization introduces a product or service improvement, its rivals copy it – sometimes within days. The result, as Paul Goldberger, chief cultural correspondent of the *New York Times*, says, is that 'while everything may be better, it is also increasingly the same'. Management writer Tom Peters puts it more emotionally: 'a blight of sameness'.

Cars are now much more reliable than ever before, but they also have much less personality. There are exceptions, of course: a Ferrari is still a Ferrari. But if you compare cars in terms of the mass-market, they're hard to tell apart. Put three family saloons side by side, and remove the makers' badges, and you'll find it hard to say which is which.

As soon as one airline offers you a lie-down bed in business class, market forces come into play, and all the other airlines offer you the same thing.

Compare the weekend broadsheet newspapers in Britain. They all have eight or nine different sections, and they all cover exactly the same ground. The sections even have the same titles: 'weekend', 'review' and so on. The lack of originality is depressing.

One supermarket chain introduces a new service feature – for instance, a promise that if the checkout queue in front of you has more than three people in it, they'll open an extra checkout desk. Within weeks, all the supermarkets offer the same thing.

Even sophisticated firms like accountants are hard to tell apart: surveys show that clients can detect very little difference between, for example, the big five accounting firms.

And this blight of sameness has spread into politics too. In too many Western democracies, the mainstream political parties offer uncannily similar policies. As people become more prosperous, their interests converge. Old oppositions between, for example, capital and labour mean less. So canny politicians make a bland appeal to the increasingly large middle ground.

And sameness is nowhere more apparent than on the internet, where there are so few variables between one website experience and another. There's nothing to touch, smell or taste, no shops to wander through, no theme parks to explore, no cafés to sample in the endless sameness of cyberspace.

And even when companies do think carefully about the 'experiences' they offer customers, the result can still be bland or unsatisfactory.

For example, Tom Peters calls the particular kind of customer service you get at Ritz-Carlton hotels 'the Ritz-Carlton pause'. He reports that every staff member he encountered 'took a couple of seconds, stopped, looked me in the eye, and asked "How's everything going? Is there anything I can do for you?"' Peters claims that this level of customer service is hard to copy. 'You could duplicate all that brass and marble, duplicate the award-winning architect's design . . . and, with a friendly banker or two, duplicate the great location. But copy the Ritz-Carlton pause? Damn near impossible.'

But is it really a source of long-term competitive advantage?

These special kinds of experience are hard to deliver consistently. Many people have stayed in Ritz-Carlton hotels without experiencing the Ritz-Carlton pause. Some have found that, though staff are keen to help, they don't always follow through. Others have found that, though the staff are friendly, the hotel spaces themselves are bland and dull. They represent a rather old-fashioned view of the kinds of spaces that business people find reassuring or flattering – wood panelling, old prints, a club feel – that may not be Ritz-Carlton's, or anyone else's, future.

And some kinds of special experience are not hard to copy. You could, in principle, train staff in any hotel to do 'the Ritz-Carlton pause' routine.

What's worse, experiences may be superficial or

artificial. Some guests may find this kind of service delightful; others irritating. Do you really want to be stopped every five minutes and asked how everything's going? This can easily look like a kind of fake glossiness, a set of behaviours learned by rote. It may work well in the United States, but feel far too familiar for guests in Europe or Asia Pacific. Consumers will increasingly demand more than a Ritz-Carlton pause: they'll want to be able to detect, and take part in, a bigger idea that underlies it.

Even a widely admired company like Starbucks comes under criticism for creating too bland an experience. British design guru Stephen Bayley claims that 'it's a sort of an illusion of choice that is being offered, rather than real choice'. Starbucks, he complains, 'are offering a higher level of beverage, but there is something slightly sinister about it, because they offer a simulacrum of domesticity and intimacy – but you really are just being manipulated by a large corporation'.

In the developed world, then, there's now plenty of choice, but with plenty of choice has come plenty of sameness. With the rise of quality and the rise of customer service has come the rise of blandness. There's a search for something more.

People feel a deep sense of *ennui*. At last, we have everything we need: and we find we actually want more. Not more consumption, but something beyond consumption. In the developed world, where there's lots of choice among many good things, people are starting to echo King Lear's cry, 'reason not the need'.

In a 1998 Gallup survey, 77 per cent of people felt that they had no material comforts missing from their lives. What we all want now is something that goes deeper.

The psychologists say that we're shifting from being 'sustenance-driven' (looking for basic needs to be met) through being 'outer-directed' (looking for esteem and status) to being 'inner-directed' (looking for self-fulfilment). But it's more complicated than that: the search for self-fulfilment is a collective, not an individual, search. We don't want to find our own private heaven, but to belong to something bigger – to join and contribute to a socially-validated idea.

People are looking for ideas – ideas that transform a high-quality product or a well-delivered service into something more. Ideas that rebel against sameness. Ideas that are about more than just *need*.

Consumers with attitude

Who's leading this rebellion against sameness? A new kind of consumer. Consumers now have more information and therefore more power than ever before. 'We're seeing a fundamental shift of power to the customer,' says Andrew Armishaw, until recently chief executive at First Direct.

Terry Leahy, chief executive of the supermarket chain Tesco, sees exactly the same thing. The shift is happening for a whole range of reasons. 'Because in certain areas there's more supply than demand. Because of privatization. Because barriers to world trade are coming down. Because of education, experience, travel. And because consumers are more aware of their own power and currency.'

In a way, this is nothing new: ever since the rise of consumerism in the 1960s, people have taken a much deeper and more sceptical interest in what's being sold to them.

But in the last couple of years, the internet has accelerated things dramatically. People used to have to trudge around the shops, or at least make dozens of phonecalls, to compare rival offers: now they can find the best deal for almost anything in just a few minutes on the internet. Even better, there are programs and websites to do the searching for them.

And beyond that, consumers are now setting the price for what they buy. Dozens of websites allow consumers to name the price they want to pay for an air ticket, a hotel room, a car, or almost anything. Suddenly, it's the suppliers, not the buyers, who have to do the running around.

This shift means that today's consumer is not only infinitely better informed. There's also, in Armishaw's words, 'a new attitude: customers no longer respect authority'.

The age of deference is over: an era of almost militant democratization is beginning. 'Individuals', says Andrew Armishaw, 'are exerting their authority in society. They're saying "I'm owed this", though not, in a 1980s way, at other people's expense.'

They're saying this across the whole range of decisions they make. Not just which airline to fly, but which school is best for their children, which charity makes the best use of their donations, which politician should run the country.

From welfare services, refuse collectors, passport issuers, the police, they're demanding more than they currently get.

Political decisions, more than ever, are economic more

than ideological. People ask: 'which politician will spend my taxes on the things I'd most like to spend them on?' This thinking isn't necessarily selfish, but it's self-assured. It's not about which option is best for my narrow self-interest. Instead, it's about which option best reflects the kind of person I want to be.

From a world in which organizations (including political parties) make things and then sell them to as many people as they can, we're entering a world in which buyers actively seek out those things that resonate for them, those things that they can identify with.

From a world in which sellers set the price, we're moving towards a world where buyers say what they're prepared to pay.

From a world in which manufacturers make and consumers consume, we're arriving in a world in which buyers participate in shared endeavours. In fact, it's a world where the very word 'consumer' no longer makes much sense.

We're moving from a world of selling to a world of buying.

It's not about pushing things out to people. It's not about bright and breezy sales messages, which everyone can now see through. It's about attracting people in, so that they can then pull out the things they want.

Emotional magnet

All of which means that organizations need a magnet – something to bring people in, and to make them stay around.

That magnet has to be more than quality, more than

service: those are assumed, expected, taken for granted. They're a minimum, a starting point.

Organizations need to propose a whole emotional world: something people can react to, something they can choose to reject or to join. With plenty of attitude themselves, consumers warm to organizations that themselves have attitude.

And, as the heart of this emotional world, people are looking for a big idea.

The big idea can be old, like 'democracy', or new, like 'usability', or timeless, like 'purity'. But those organizations that can attach themselves to an idea like this gain an immensely powerful emotional magnet.

Instead of limiting themselves to an old-world category like 'clothing retailer' or 'computer company' or 'cosmetics maker', they open themselves up to the expansive possibilities suggested by their big idea. They win a huge advantage in the 'what's next?' world.

Orange, for instance, is about much more than mobile phones; it's about optimism. Saturn is about much more than cars: it's about harmony. Sony is about much more than electronics: it's about miniature perfection.

The idea doesn't need to be about newness or novelty, though it can be. It needn't be about history or tradition, although these can be potent. What it must do is excite and inspire people. It must answer their craving for a new kind of experience. It must suggest that, by making a relationship with this particular organization, they're entering a different world, a new order, something better. It must show that, in choosing this particular organization, they won't get the same bland product or service that everyone else gets.

It's not that the organization is selling them a mortgage

or a plane ticket: it's more that they're joining a world of irreverence, or rigour, or winning, or whatever the idea may be. It's a world they like, feel at home in, want to be part of. It's a world that makes them feel good, and to which they can contribute.

In this new marketplace, many conventional distinctions start to lose meaning. In the past, charities stood for good causes, while commercial organizations simply made money. Now, any organization can pursue a worthwhile big idea. Any organization can seek to make the world a better place. Indeed, increasingly, every organization must seek to make the world a better place – or it won't attract the best customers, the best employees and the best investors. The line between hard capitalism and soft, do-good charities is now harder to maintain.

Big ideas like this aren't an entirely new phenomenon. Charities and pressure groups have had big ideas for a hundred years or more. Enlightened capitalists like the Quakers pursued more than short-term commercial goals. And an organization like Britain's National Health Service was created with the huge and inspiring big idea of providing free health care for everyone.

But amid the frenzy of 'what's next?', the battle is on to find the biggest ideas. For government bodies, private charities, non-governmental organizations, start-up companies and multinational corporations, the search is on for a big enough idea – big enough to sustain the corporation through uncharted waters, big enough to inspire new possibilities, new ventures, new directions. Organizations with no visible big idea are looking for one. Those that started life with a big idea are seeking to rediscover it, to redefine it in contemporary terms – something the NHS needs to do, for instance – in order to survive. The age of 'what's next?' demands open-minded, original and strongly felt thinking: it's the age of the big idea.

CHAPTER TWO

values for money

In this feverish, but immensely exciting, marketplace, the consumer-with-attitude is looking for something new. Not value for money, but *values for money*.

Money is less tangible than it's ever been: it's not bullion but binary digits. Yet, of course, it's just as emotionally important. And what people want in exchange for their money is more than the merely tangible, more than just the functional, more than a fair economic swap: more, even, than good quality or great service.

Of course, consumers still compare prices and assess product features. They expect quality and service. But increasingly, they focus not on the features they can touch, but on the intangible something behind them. And that ethereal something has become even more urgently relevant in the internet economy, since the internet is itself so ethereal.

Consumers talking in focus groups about the choices they make – between different credit cards, for instance – often start by concentrating on variations in interest rates or in loyalty schemes. But it soon emerges that many of them don't really know what the interest rate is, or how the loyalty scheme works. Shyly at first, they talk about less rational aspects of the credit card – its design, its advertising campaign, the things it seems to stand for. And suddenly, everyone is enthusing: these are the real drivers of consumer choice.

People look for the things they can identify with, the things they'd like to be part of, the things that make them feel better about themselves. In the 'what's next?' marketplace, values matter most.

And values matter not just in the commercial marketplace. People want values from the way their taxes are spent, or the way their charitable donations are put to use. They want much more than just efficiency.

In every field, people look beyond old-fashioned 'value for money' to something much more complex, much more intriguing: *values* for money.

We think this is for you

The first plea is a simple one: help me. Get on my side. Share my values. Guide me towards the things I'll like.

It's a bewildering marketplace. In the uproar of 'what's next?', we become engulfed in daily noise. Working out, for instance, the best mobile phone tariff to choose is almost impossibly complicated. It's very hard to know which is the best deal on house insurance. And how do you choose between schools or hospitals? Or which charity to support? These aren't idle questions, or matters of intellectual curiosity. They're matters of real concern, real anxiety, real emotional worry.

There are huge opportunities for organizations that offer to guide people through these choices.

Retailers – at any rate, the best ones – have always understood this. John Lewis Partnership, for instance, sees its role as pre-selecting goods on the customer's behalf. It offers a lowest-price guarantee, with its motto 'never knowingly undersold'. But the internet has taken all this a dramatic step further.

New kinds of company have appeared that help consumers find the right product or service at the right price. Philip Evans and Thomas S. Wurster, in their influential book *Blown to Bits*, call these organizations 'navigators': they enable people to navigate through the marketplace and find the right book, the cheapest flight, the best mortgage. They compare one product against another, feature by feature. They can put five different mortgage offers up on the screen and let you choose the best. They raid suppliers' websites, dig out all the relevant information on competing products, and ruthlessly put all the data on the screen. Some go even further: Priceline was the first of several websites that let buyers set the price they're prepared to pay for an airline ticket, a hotel room, a mortgage, a car. An age in which purchasers, not sellers, set the price for things really is an age of the buyer.

Any field in which there's too much choice will be fertile territory for 'navigators'. One area is television. With digital television, consumers are now starting to have access to electronic programme guides that may offer them ten different gardening make-over programmes, or ten different adaptations of Agatha Christie. Organizations like the BBC want to make their own programmes stand out, so that viewers think 'the BBC's version is the version I trust, and that's the one I'll choose'. 'The critical thing for the BBC', says its sales and marketing director, Jane Frost, 'is to use people's immense emotional bond with the BBC to make its work stand out in, for example, an electronic programme guide.'

'Consumers face an avalanche of choice,' says Michael

Jackson, chief executive of television company Channel 4. He sees his company's role as changing profoundly. When there were just four television channels, Channel 4 acted as one of four gatekeepers, jointly dictating what the nation could and could not watch. 'Now', says Jackson, 'we're becoming a choice editor, saying "we think this is for you".' In other words, Channel 4 is changing from providing a channel to endorsing particular programmes – from selling to helping people buy. Organizations that do this, says Jackson, 'will have the power in the marketplace'.

The demand, then, is for organizations to become navigators: to cross the divide between seller and buyer, to put themselves on the consumer's side. Easily said, but not easily done: for most organizations, this means throwing away decades of self-protective practices and instincts. It's not simple for a government agency to switch sides and champion the citizen. It's not easy for a hospital to side with the patients rather than the doctors. It's not easy for a bank to cut unnecessary charges and delete advantageous small print. Above all, it's extremely hard for an organization to reach the logical conclusion of all this and, when a rival's product is better than its own, to sell that rival product instead. But there are plenty of pressures driving organizations towards this conclusion.

Alongside this, any organization that wants to be a 'navigator' faces a parallel challenge: it has to win the trust of its consumers. For consumers-with-attitude to consent to follow a navigator, they have to trust that navigator, and trust them deeply.

Becoming a navigator isn't a matter of efficiently scouring markets and finding the best deals, important though that is. Much more crucially, it's about establishing an affinity with customers. It's about making them feel that its choices are the choices they would make themselves.

The best navigators – people like John Lewis in the traditional economy and Amazon in the new one – are, to their customers, 'people like us'. John Lewis is much more than 'never knowingly undersold': it creates a climate in which customers feel that the store is emotionally on their side, that it shares their values. Amazon carefully fosters a sense that it's as passionate about books, CDs, DVDs and so on as its customers. These navigators offer values for money.

To build affinity, an organization has to be selective. It has to decide who it wants as its constituency. It has to be clear whose values it shares. People need to know what it likes and dislikes, what it's for and against. It can't be all things to all people. It must stand for something.

Making natural life possible

In a complicated marketplace, people want guides and navigators. But they want more. Reacting against the blight of sameness, they're looking for distinctiveness. Awash with plenty, they're looking for rarity. Surrounded by the mass-produced, they demand the hand-made. With copies everywhere, they want the original. And with the population in most developed countries getting older, the cult of youth is starting to wane: more value will be attached to experience, less to novelty: more to reality, less to image.

People are in search of authenticity.

'There's enough products in the world,' observes Anders Knutsen, of Danish hi-fi maker Bang & Olufsen. 'People don't want products but dreams.' Rolf Jensen, in his book *The Dream Society*, makes the same point. He says consumers are looking for a story. For example, when they choose free-range eggs, consumers 'are happy to pay an additional 15 to 20 per cent for the story behind the egg. They are willing to pay more for the story about animal ethics, about rustic romanticism, about the good old days . . . Both kinds of eggs are similar in quality, but consumers prefer the egg with the better story.'

'There will be a rebellion against homogeneity,' predicts Alan Rusbridger, editor of Britain's *Guardian* newspaper. He sees the Millennium Dome in London as the nadir of a kind of bland, homogeneous culture, a temple of empty experience, a place without an idea.

This search for the authentic is, of course, nothing new. The eighteenth-century poet Edward Young put the plea simply: 'Born Originals, how comes it to pass that we die Copies?' And a hundred years ago, Oscar Wilde predicted a motto for the twentieth century: 'Over the portal of the new world "Be thyself" shall be written.' But this search has been intensified by the era of mass production – the technique that helped create the new world of choice and sameness in which we live.

'When the first Ford automobiles came rolling off the assembly line,' says trend-watcher Faith Popcorn, 'shiny, smooth, and, above all, all the same, the world came to see uniformity . . . as the mark of excellence for the modern age. Now the very reverse is coming to be true. Smooth, shiny and uniform is often now equated with crude and cheap, especially when compared with the individuality of hand-crafted (or somehow individually crafted) products.'

And globalization hasn't helped. 'The branded multinationals may talk diversity', says journalist Naomi Klein, 'but the visible result of their actions is an army of teen clones marching – in "uniform", as the marketeers say – into the global mall. Despite the embrace of polyethnic imagery, market-driven globalization doesn't want diversity; quite the opposite.'

The search for the hand-crafted has a paradox behind it. We want what's authentic – real, true, special, rare – but we all want it. So what the planet needs as a whole is rarity, in vast quantities. The paradox becomes particularly clear when you talk to the people who make that modern (and ancient) necessity, wine. Bruce Kemp is the man who turned Australia's Southcorp into one of the world's biggest makers of premium wine – the people behind Lindemans, Penfolds and many other brands.

'Consumers', he says, 'will continue to want diversity in wine – a broad and very long piece of cloth. Particularly with the web, they'll be more knowledgeable – there will be a hunger for information.' So people will be better informed, and will want unusual, distinctive, different wines from smaller winemakers. But 'at the same time, there'll be huge chains of wine retailers – look at Wal-Mart and Asda – that can place orders of a quarter of a million cases: a scale of demand that eliminates 90 per cent of the world's wine companies.' People want diversity, distinctiveness, rarity – yet they want it in huge quantities.

To put it another way, we want individuality, but we expect consistency too – many different experiences from the same organization, with a guarantee that none of those experiences will be disappointing. It's a tricky balance between predictability and unpredictability, between safety and risk.

One way to be authentic is to strip down your product or service, to cut out the frills, to celebrate the *functional*. Direct Line insurance in the UK, and Charles Schwab in the USA, are two financial services organizations that have stripped out the inessentials and offer lower insurance premiums, or lower share-dealing fees, than their rivals. But their appeal goes beyond the merely functional: they attract people who take a pride in getting a good deal. Direct Line and Charles Schwab are about attitude.

The next step beyond that is to put even more fun in functional, by making functional equate to stylish. The Japanese retailer Muji sells 'no brand' products – clothes and household things that have no logos on them. Their products are deliberately simple, plain, undecorated, functional. And yet the appeal of Muji isn't a rational appeal – Muji invites people to join it in a search for simplicity, an escape from the hothouse of fashion brands. 'As society is becoming more uniform', says its recently retired president, Ariga Kaoru, 'young people will build lifestyles on their own values. Muji is very well prepared because we provide the basics on which people build lifestyles.' Muji is about attitude, too.

And beyond even Muji are companies that make the functional seem not just stylish but politically correct – like the Body Shop – or even ethically pure. The 1990s saw a huge rise in the popularity of furniture made to the designs of the Shaker communities of New England. Rarely has a religious sect been used so successfully to give a moral dimension to a household product.

All these businesses emphasize the functional side of what they do. But they do it in a way that appeals to people's sense of the rightness of being plain.

This search for the authentic is nowhere clearer than in

food. Ten years ago, organic food looked like one of the weirdest of food fads. Now it's the fastest growing segment in Western supermarkets. What's driving the soaring demand for organic food?

The organization at the centre of organic farming in Britain is the Soil Association, a club of farmers set up in the 1940s, and its director, Patrick Holden, has a simple answer: the failure of homogenization.

Since the Second World War, agribusiness has produced plentiful amounts of consistent, predictable, apparently high-quality food. But consumers have begun to feel there's a price to pay, that this food is full of lurking and mysterious danger. They've seen salmonella from factory-farmed chickens, and BSE from factory-farmed cattle. People have become scared of additives, and concerned about geneti-cally-modified ingredients.

In the face of this fear, this negativity, organic food pro-vides a hugely welcome positive. Rather than fleeing from science, consumers are hastening towards nature. Organic farming offers something that's not just safer, it's more natural, more *authentic*. People are prepared, almost para-doxically, to pay more for food *without* additives. This real food, they believe, is better for you, better for the environ-ment, and tastes better too.

And beneath all this, Patrick Holden believes, lies a deeper, unspoken search: a search for wholeness. People have become used to thinking of health as an absence of sickness: the key to health is drugs that combat disease. But there's another view in which health is a state in its own right, and the key to health is good nutritious food. What matters is not clever scientific intervention, but original natural wholeness.

'This isn't understood intellectually but it's intrinsically felt by people,' says Patrick Holden. 'More generally people want to find their identity, their roots, their sense of relatedness to landscape. There's a sense that we're distorting the harmonic order with our heavy-handed acts, making natural life impossible.'

And Patrick Holden goes further: 'Some people believe that there's an inaudible harmony in nature, that nature and music are very close.' This starts to feel like a flakey and esoteric theory: but that's the fascination of organic food. In this world, sound common sense shades imperceptibly into new-age mysticism. But that shading matters: it hints that there's a spiritual dimension, not often examined or discussed or analysed, in the day-to-day decisions of the new consumer.

So the hunt is on for the authentic. Any organization that's going to deliver authenticity must be true to itself. It must reject the bland, the artificial, the fake. It must stand out for what's real.

Buying virtue

And there's another strand to the fabric of 'values for money'. In addition to guidance and navigation, in addition to authenticity, we want to be good. What we buy is virtue.

And we want to feel that the people we buy from are good too: otherwise, we become tainted ourselves. 'As consumers seek to be "the best they can be"', says Elsie Maio in her essay 'The Next Wave', 'they are attracted to businesses that do the same.'

And 'taint' is the right word. These aren't carefully considered ethical decisions by consumers: it's all done on feel. As Tom Peters says, '70 per cent of customers bail out because of the look/feel/smell/taste of doing business with a company.'

Never before have we looked so closely at the source of the things we buy – the people behind the products, their priorities, their methods, the things they stand for. This is an age of unparalleled organizational scrutiny.

The last two decades of the twentieth century saw corporation after corporation failing to be its best: a Union Carbide pesticide plant killing 4000 in 1984, Sandoz flooding toxic chemicals into the Rhine in 1986, the Exxon Valdez supertanker oil spill in 1989, Shell's problems with its Brent Spar oil platform, and with human rights in Nigeria, in 1995. And so on.

Sir Stuart Hampson at John Lewis Partnership says, 'customers will expect things of businesses that are over and above pure commercial considerations. They'll ask: what is your stance on ethical trading or environmental support? People want to know what our supermarkets think about genetically-modified products: it's part of their decision-making process.' Consumers want to know what companies *think* about things.

In other words, people want the right product or the right service, but they want something else too: they want to know that there's an organization behind it that thinks rather in the way they think, or even that's ahead of their thinking. They want an organization that shares their worries, that stands for what they stand for.

As Sir Mark Moody-Stuart, chairman of Shell, says, 'people all need energy – but need other things as well. They need personal transportation, it's hugely liberating:

that "Hey for the open road" feeling is still important in developing countries. But then they also worry about the effect on the climate, the problems of pollution and congestion. They say "It's going to take me three hours to drive across Mumbai".'

Two-thirds of respondents to a survey in the USA said they would switch brands to a manufacturer that supported a cause they deemed worthwhile. In another survey, 83 per cent of respondents said they prefer buying environmentally-safe products.

And in some cases, people are prepared to pay more for this extra dimension – they'll pay a premium to buy something from a company that feels the same way they do, that worries about the same things. A new electricity company, UNIT[e], was launched in Britain in autumn 1999, selling energy derived purely from renewable sources such as wind farms – and charging up to ten per cent more.

And investors are becoming as concerned as consumers with the ethics of the companies they invest in. Ethical investment funds are soaring. In the United States, one out of every eight investment dollars is now in some kind of 'socially responsible' fund – and investment in these funds is growing twice as fast as the wider market.

There are now four stockmarket indexes that track 'sustainable' businesses: the Domini 400 Social Index in the USA, the NPI Social Index in Britain, the Jantzi Social Index in Canada, and the Dow Jones Sustainability Group Index for international shares. This last index tracks 250 businesses – those that take their environmental responsibilities most seriously, according to the index's elaborate scoring system. These 250 are an odd collection, but the top scorers include BMW, Fuji Film, Unilever, Bristol-Myers Squibb, Credit Suisse and Fujitsu. Three of these indexes – the Domini 400, the NPI and the Dow Jones Sustainability Group – have been around long enough to build up a track record. All three have outperformed their ethically neutral counterparts.

Increasingly, organizations are finding it worthwhile to report not just their financial performance, but also their environmental effectiveness. Environmental reporting is becoming more and more common in business. According to a study by the Institute for Environmental Management and the accounting firm KPMG, 35 per cent of the world's 250 largest corporations now issue environmental reports.

All of this applies now to companies who the public believe have a direct impact on health or the environment – to foods companies, pharmaceuticals and biotechnology businesses and energy suppliers. But it will soon apply to every company, Thomas Wellauer, chief executive of Credit Suisse Financial Services, believes that 'every consumer-facing business will need to stand for something beyond the service it offers'.

Standing for something

This idea of 'standing for something' is critical in the values-for-money marketplace.

In choosing a navigator, people look for organizations that stand for what they stand for, that make the choices they'd make. In searching for authenticity, people prefer those organizations that stand for rarity, purity, natural ingredients. And in their constant ethical scrutiny, people pick out those organizations that stand firm on certain principles, that will sacrifice short-term commercial gains in the interests of doing the right thing.

In all of these ways, organizations that *stand for* something *stand out*.

But at the same time that they seek out products and services that stand for what they believe in, people are returning to the old idea of value-for-money. Indeed, value-for-money has itself become rather a chic idea – it's good to get a bargain, and to be seen to get a bargain. As Barbara Cassani, chief executive of Go, the low-cost airline from British Airways, says: 'there's a new culture in which it's smart to get things at a good price – like Gap for instance'. This new culture plays into the hands of airlines like Go and Southwest. It drives the sales of fashionable small cars like the Smart car or the Ford Ka. It works for financial services firms that offer better interest rates or lower fees. It helps supermarkets sell their own-label products.

But this isn't the same as old-fashioned value for money. People will buy these lower-cost products and services only if the emotions are right too – only if they feel Gap speaks to them, that Go is their kind of airline, that they love the look of the Ford Ka, or that their supermarket is taking the right stand on genetically-modified food. It's not 'if the price is right, I'll buy', it's 'if the product or service is right, I'm happy to take advantage of the lower price too'. This really is *values for money*.

Beneath this kind of decision-making lies something deeper. In the open-ended, unsettling, agnostic 'what's next?' world, people are searching for belief. While enjoying the maelstrom, people also want to feel connected to an anchor or two. People want things they can believe in.

This doesn't mean falling blindly for certain attractive brands. It means selecting, with eyes wide open, some organizations, and rejecting others. Increasingly, people are drawn to organizations that inspire, not blind loyalty, but a deeper belief.

This redoubles the need for an organization to have a big idea. To stand for something. To offer something worth believing in.

When the future's uncertain, it might be something as simple as Orange's idea of 'optimism'. When there's an impossibly large choice of books in print, it might be Amazon's idea about 'completeness'. When industrial farming has come under question, it might be something like the Soil Association's idea about 'organics', or Ben & Jerry's idea about 'home-made'. Whatever it is, the militant consumer is waiting not just to buy, but to *buy in*.

CHAPTER THREE

the end of inside

It's a world of 'what's next?', where anything's possible, where an organization can, in principle, do anything. And it's world of values for money, where people want organizations – whatever it is they do – to stand for something.

In the face of all that, perhaps not surprisingly, organizations are changing: changing beyond recognition. Indeed, they're ceasing to be organizations in the traditional sense – well-defined entities with a clear boundary operating in a particular arena. They're becoming something much more fluid, much looser, much harder to grasp, but much more exciting to live in.

Old borderlines are evaporating, old categories are merging. The divisions between commercial, public-sector and non-profit organizations are becoming blurred. All organizations now act on the same stage, and need to justify their place on that stage.

At the same time, the distinctions between customers, employees, suppliers and investors are becoming blurred: customers are also employees, employees are also shareholders, competitors are also suppliers. All organizations need to speak with one voice to all their stakeholders – or quickly get caught out as two-faced.

All of which adds up to a new imperative for every organization. Whether they're a big corporation, a small start-up, a school, a hospital or a charity, they can no longer make trade-offs between their stakeholder groups. They need an idea big enough to unite all their stakeholders – and not just unite them, but excite them too. They need to stand for something beyond narrow commercial goals. Something that resonates not just with customers, but with investors and employees – and with the media, government regulators, environmental pressure groups, and whoever else could decide their fate. To do all that, the idea must be simple, compelling and emotional.

Who's who?

One of the world's largest organizations is running an advertising campaign on human rights. They talk about how they're 'committed to support fundamental human rights' and about how they've 'spoken out on the rights of individuals – even when the situation has been beyond their control'. Who is this? One of the world's great aid charities, like Oxfam? No, it's a multinational energy company – Shell.

Another of the world's most powerful organizations exists outside government. It operates internationally, to its own agenda. It's unclear exactly who it's accountable to. It has changed the goals and methods of an agency as prestigious as the World Bank. Who is this? A sinister multinational? No, it's the consortium of non-governmental organizations that ran the 'Fifty Years is Enough' campaign against the World Bank in its half-centenary year, 1994.

And one of the most successful software products of the moment is an operating system called Linux. It has 12 million users worldwide. Who makes it? IBM? No, a loose federation of 750,000 software experts, most of whom design it and develop it in their own spare time. And if you want to buy it, you can't: it's free.

This is indeed a strange world, where multinationals champion human rights, where NGOs are the new economic influencers, and where a huge club of enthusiasts makes a valuable product just for the love of it.

Charities now realize that giving isn't purely altruistic, that they offer a service to customers, and that donors expect to get something back. Public agencies now realize that, though they may have no direct competitors, their quality of service is judged against other, more commercial service providers.

Some public agencies are, at the same time, also commercial enterprises and charities. The British Council, which promotes British culture around the world, also runs money-making English-language schools. It's simultaneously a government agency, a business and an educational charity.

Other public agencies are getting increasingly close to the private NGOs. The World Bank, having been attacked by NGOs in the mid 1990s, is now embracing them. 'From environmental policy to debt relief,' reports *The Economist*, 'NGOs are at the centre of World Bank policy. Often they determine it.'

And increasingly, public and private enterprises are working together as virtual organizations. Much of Britain's welfare-to-work programme, for example, is run in this way, with two government departments, hundreds of local government authorities, and a set of welfare charities and private-sector service providers all operating as one. Across the world, it will become increasingly rare for public services to be delivered by organizations that are purely publicly-owned.

These examples are early signs of a huge change in the landscape.

It's a change which recognizes something that's always been true. When you take into account housework, government programmes, charities, agencies and clubs, most of the work done every day on the planet isn't for commercial ends. It's a change which means that the world's stock-markets are no longer the home of all significant 'commercial' activity. Above all, it's a loosening up of human enterprise, an end to rigid distinctions.

What's happened so far is that non-commercial organizations have emulated the private sector. Almost all organizations – public sector, private sector or so-called third sector (charities) – now have chief executives, strategic plans and marketing departments. Almost all talk about their 'customers'. Benefits claimants, university students, art-gallery visitors, bus passengers: these days all are treated as customers. Universities and charities now talk very seriously about 'market share'.

What will happen next is a flow of thinking in the other direction. Commercial organizations will realize that most public and non-profit agencies have something they desperately need: a significant purpose.

Businesses in the last two decades of the old century were dominated by the idea of shareholder value, and that ethos was in large part taken up by public agencies and non-profit organizations too. In the new century, it's different. The goal isn't shareholder value. For every kind of organization, it's a purpose beyond profit.

It's true that privatization has brought many public

enterprises into the world's stock markets. But these new arrivals merely highlight the fact that all commercial organizations serve more than just their owners. Indeed, most newly privatized companies are forced – through increasingly stringent government regulation – to aim for more goals than short-term profit. But in addition, public and media pressure on, for instance, Britain's railway companies, is much more strenuous and indignant than it ever was in the days before privatization.

Public moral pressure on everyone from Monsanto to Nike to Coca-Cola has never been greater. Indeed, *Newsweek* detects a new agenda here. 'Since the cold war', it says, 'most of the social debate has been about the privatization of the public sector. The new agenda seems to be the reverse: *public-ization* of the private sector.'

No compartments

It's not just the barriers between sectors that are coming down. The border around each individual organization is evaporating too. In the era of the internet, it's very hard for an organization to defend its edges, to maintain a clear distinction between what's inside and what's outside. Information flows freely. Through email, customers and employees can talk without supervision. And organizations are coming under intense and increasing consumer scrutiny.

Commercial or non-profit, public or private, every organization now has to deal with a multiplicity of stakeholder groups. These groups include the people who provide the money: owners, investors, members, grant-giving bodies, donors or taxpayers. Then the people who provide services to the organization: suppliers, consultants and out-sourcers. The people who do the work: employees, future employees, former employees. The people who take the product or service to customers: distributors, retailers, brokers, agents and intermediaries. The people who receive the organization's products or services: customers or beneficiaries. And the wider public, influenced by the media and by campaigners.

These stakeholder groups, of course, have conflicting interests. And in a way, managing an organization has in the past been largely about making successful trade-offs between those interests. Crudely, you help one group by harming another. This has led to a spirit of divide and rule: keep the groups separate, and keep them all happy by selling a subtly different message to each group.

But now it's more complicated, because these stakeholder groups increasingly overlap.

For large organizations, many customers are also employees – that's always been the case. But now that both groups are more self-aware and assertive, it matters more. Fast food companies, for instance, find that the very things that appeal to customers put off staff. For example, Carmel Flattley, chief HR and training officer for McDonald's, says, 'Value pricing seemed to equate to low pay and low-calibre jobs, while consistency of product translated to little opportunity for initiative and innovation.'

For many commercial companies, customers are now shareholders too. In America, half of all households now contain stockmarket investors – either through the new craze of trading shares over the internet or, more likely, through holding mutual funds (unit trusts in Britain). In a way that's good: shareholder-customers want their business to succeed. But it also means that shareholders are adopting the new, tougher attitudes of the consumer. Just as consumers out shopping want to be sure that T-shirt wasn't made by exploited children, and that aubergine isn't genetically modified, so investors want to know what exactly they're putting their money into.

And increasingly employees are shareholders. Employee share schemes are now widely seen as a way of helping employees see the business from a shareholder's point of view, and act as if they were owners.

Suppliers are also becoming shareholders, particularly for small, start-up businesses. Unable to afford the fees of their professional advisers, start-ups are offering stock to their lawyers, accountants, bankers and consultants, and an increasingly elaborate web of ownership is proliferating.

At the same time, it's becoming hard to tell suppliers and employees apart, as organizations transfer more and more of their own work to specialist outsourcing companies. When you check in to fly on Go, the low-cost airline founded by British Airways, you're greeted by people who seem to be the embodiment of Go: young, friendly, informal and non-deferential. Yet they're not actually employees, because Go outsources its baggage handling.

In a way, these baggage-handlers are intermediaries – brokers between an organization and its customers. This is becoming a much more common role: not just for familiar people like the insurance broker, but also the huge new area of customer call centres, where telephonists employed by a specialist call centre company impersonate the organization you think you're calling. It's almost impossible for customers to tell who works for who – and it's sometimes confusing for staff too.

And increasingly, companies, their suppliers and their customers are using exactly the same computer system – the internet. Ford and GM, for example, are both connecting their suppliers, business partners and customers into one huge electronic market. This is great for customers, who will be able to order exactly the car they want, have it built to order, and track its progress through the factory. But it also means that the organizations involved all see the same data, on the same computer system: it's getting very hard these days to keep secrets.

Some observers think the time for secrets has passed, anyway, and that organizations need to enlist the skills of all their stakeholders – including customers. The management experts C. K. Prahalad and Venkatram Ramaswamy believe that customers are an important source of what they call 'competence', and that organizations need therefore to bring customers inside their organizational system. 'The recognition that consumers are a source of competence', they say, 'forces managers to cast an even wider net: competence now is a function of the collective knowledge available to the whole system – an enhanced network of traditional suppliers, manufacturers, partners, investors, *and* customers.'

So organizations are emerging whose boundaries are very hard to define. Most people fall into more than one 'stakeholder' category: they have more than one stake in the business. And many people fall both inside and outside the organization: they're both customers and employees, they're outsourcers posing as employees, they're suppliers who own part of the business – and so on.

In effect, it's the end of 'inside'.

Independent belonging

At the same time as organizations are becoming more fluid, the people in and around them want more than ever to *belong*. After two decades of rampant individualism, the idea of community has again become attractive. But this isn't a return to collectivism. People want to belong, but not to be subsumed. They want to join communities of individuals: communities that will enhance, rather than submerge, their sense of themselves.

There's a growing desire among all the stakeholders of the organization to engage, contribute, participate – not simply to be 'employees', whose role is merely to be employed, or 'consumers', whose role is merely to consume.

And increasingly people are forming lateral relationships. Through email in particular, workers can now compare notes instantly with colleagues all over the world. And customers can share with each other their pleasure in, or their dissatisfaction with, any organization they're interested in.

All of this is turning 'organization' into 'community'.

For employees, the desire to belong without being subsumed is changing their relationship with organizations. They're moving from one allegiance – a job for life – to many. They are sharing out their time among those organizations, big or small, that mean most to them.

Until relatively recently, most workers had a 'career'. Most people joined an organization – public sector, private sector or non-profit – and stayed with it, or at least stayed in that sector, through their lives. People used to feel loyal to their organization simply because it employed them: its future and their own future were inextricably bound. Big companies, of course, still exist, and are getting bigger. But in the USA and Britain, and increasingly in the rest of Europe and Japan, the traditional relationship between organization and employee has disappeared.

More people change job more often. People – particularly the so-called 'knowledge workers' – are far more aware of their economic value.

More people retire early. But conversely, as the supply of younger workers dries up, more older people will choose to go back into work. More people become freelancers through choice or necessity. Now that capital isn't hard to raise, it's much easier to set up on your own. In 1985, one British worker in ten was self-employed. By 2005, that figure will be one in seven.

All of this has changed the whole feel of working. People are prepared to do different things, either over time or at the same time.

Because people are now more consciously dividing their allegiance, they're much more demanding of these organizations they give their allegiance to. They want to belong, but on their own terms. For some, the money may be unimportant. Older people returning to work, for example: what will entice them back?

And people are less ready to sign themselves over to the organization that employs them. This need for independence is confirmed by Sir John Browne at BP. 'At the high end of the employment market', he says, 'we have to attract more than our fair share of good people, a disproportionately fair share. So the important questions become: how does it feel inside this company? how am I going to have my own self-determination?'

The decline of 'company man' has left employees almost frighteningly free. As Charles Handy says, 'We, the individuals, aren't ownable any more. As all the traditional structures disappear, we all inevitably become responsible for ourselves, more completely than ever before. We are "condemned to be free".' This underlying sense of freedom – this demand for self-determination – is the most important factor in the new relationship between organization and employee.

Which may all be fine for high-powered oil company executives and for highly-paid management consultants. But isn't work for most people still just a daily grind? Aren't most people grateful for any job? Is this a big problem, or just a tiny one? To answer that, look at call centres: today's equivalent of the Victorian mill. Even call centres face the same issues of attracting good people. First Direct is an example. Former chief executive Andrew Armishaw cites the kinds of questions employees now ask: 'Am I proud of it?', 'Is there fun around the place?', 'Am I treated as an individual?'

The challenge for an organization is how to marshal all this independence. The consequences of failing could be dire. 'Businesses that fail to engage the eyes, ears, minds and emotions of every individual in the organization', warns American journalist Thomas Petzinger, 'will find themselves overrun by obsolescence or crushed by competition.'

A reason beyond profit

So what makes these independent agents choose to belong to one organization over another?

They want a reason beyond profit. Profit-sharing bonuses and jam-tomorrow share option schemes have their place – and in some industries are taken for granted – but most people, on a rainy Tuesday in March, aren't highly motivated by the thought of a possible bonus cheque next December. They need something more immediate: fun, worthwhile work, self-determination, independence, values that match their own, sexiness, aggressiveness, free spirits, a big idea.

There used to be an opposition between work and everything else. But now work is becoming lifestyle. For people dividing their energies among several organizations, several projects, there's no 'weekday', no 'weekend'. More and more people are lucky enough to have jobs they enjoy.

For them, work is becoming both more important and less important. More important because work will be a central part of life – an attitude from the United States that will spread around the world. Less important because the more central it becomes, the closer to the heart of the person, the less it will feel like work. In other words, people are identifying themselves with their work and it's becoming acceptable to admit that.

'Employees are looking for values,' says Sir Stuart Hampson at John Lewis Partnership. 'People want some identity with the values of the company.' Values is an overused word, but the point is critical: workers need something that they can give themselves to, and take sustenance from.

'Most people in Europe and the US are at a level of living where all basic needs are satisfied,' says Thomas Wellauer of Credit Suisse. 'People are looking beyond money. And this is particularly true for self-motivated people, for people who want to have impact – who are, after all, the people I want to employ. They want any organization they work for to have products they admire and an idea they admire.'

This desire to belong doesn't just affect employees. Increasingly, customers too want to be part of organizations, to be active contributors rather than passive consumers.

People deciding what to do in their spare time are a good example. Britain's National Trust, which looks after 400 historic buildings and 600,000 acres of countryside, is finding that visitor numbers are levelling out, partly because the experience they offer is relatively passive, compared with a theme park or a shopping centre. 'We need to deepen the interest of our places,' says former director-general, Martin Drury. 'When there are interesting things going on, people will come. They want an experience that's dynamic, not static. People have so much choice now that one-off special events are what attracts them: they say, "let's go, here's something we might miss".'

The demand for a more active role is also detectable in public services. Governments are keen to make welfare claimants, for example, more active in pursuit of work and independence – but there are signs that the claimants themselves now expect a more active experience. The UK government's welfare-to-work scheme, ONE, has as its motto 'helping you help yourself', a thought that's not simply understood by welfare clients, but welcomed by them, as the scheme's own market research has shown.

The same approach is increasingly used by charities, keen to provide sustainable rather than one-off results to the people they work for. Britain's largest charity, Oxfam, has a commercial wing called Oxfam Moneymakers, which raises money 'to help people help themselves'.

Computer companies have for years enlisted customers in the task of getting new software right. No fewer than 650,000 customers were happy to help Microsoft, for example, to test its Windows 2000 operating system. And the internet makes this kind of dialogue much easier. 'Thanks largely to the internet', say C. K. Prahalad and Venkatram Ramaswamy, 'consumers have been increasingly engaging themselves in an active and explicit dialogue with manufacturers of products and services. What's more . . . consumers can now initiate the dialogue; they have moved out of the audience and on to the stage.'

Worth belonging to

We're just glimpsing the start of a structural shift in the nature of the organization. Most organizations today are a way of marshalling people to address outsiders within a particular part of the marketplace: a way of marshalling employees in 'business units' to meet the needs of different 'customer segments' within 'the financial services sector' or 'the telecoms sector' or 'the public sector' or 'the voluntary sector'.

But organizations are transforming into a larger, constantly changing confluence of people, interacting with each other. 'Insiders' and 'outsiders' blur together, as the organization's central nervous system extends far outside its traditional boundaries. 'Customer segments' become an artificial construct, unrelated to reality. And 'sectors' are compartments that no longer hold water: where does 'telecoms' end and 'media' start? Within this larger and looser confluence, though, there's something everyone shares:

everyone has an emotional stake in this new organization, this new community. They all belong.

It's a new kind of belonging, in which people identify themselves with an idea or an ideal – but aren't defined or subsumed by it. The community's members are volunteers, and volunteers with the power to dissent or decamp.

This picture looks strange now, but will be commonplace by mid century. Just as corporatism was the model for the twentieth century, so this kind of purposeful community will be the model for the twenty-first.

And it's a model that will apply to every kind of organization, from corner bakery to multinational conglomerate. Investors, staff and customers will all feel like owners, will all contribute, will all be beneficiaries. It's an entirely new web of relationships. The organization will tell everyone the same truth – about its successes and about the challenges facing it. And it will naturally participate in the wider world, in ways that leave a lasting impact – just as the medieval guilds (to take an earlier form of purposeful community) undertook works of charity, and put on mystery plays that are still performed today.

People will feel they belong not so much to family, church, class or nation but to the communities they participate in for food, for entertainment, for learning, for social justice – for whatever they need and believe in.

Of course most organizations today are still on the defensive. In times of trouble, they close ranks. Deep down, they see the customer as a nuisance, staff as recalcitrant, investors as people who need to be appeased.

Nevertheless, the signs of a different model are visible now.

Organizations like Apple, whose owners, staff and customers share an almost fanatical belief in doing things differently, in championing the individual. Or like John Lewis, who create a climate in which employees (who are also owners) and customers feel that they're on the same side.

Already, Apple feels like a club to its 'members'. Saturn is a club of car-owners. People feel they belong to First Direct. The Linux organization is a kind of virtual club. More and more internet services are setting up 'virtual communities' of customers who interact not just with the organization but with each other. The National Trust is a conservation agency that's also, quite literally, a membership organization.

These are the models for the future. Not an institution but a club. Not an organization but a community. Not a closed, defensive corporation with 'insiders' and 'outsiders' but an idea that all sorts of people belong to.

These examples pose a challenge for every organization. What is it that our wider community shares? What is it that all our stakeholders want to achieve? What excites all of us?

Is it better bread, or more wholesome food, or more sociable eating, or lives more fully lived?

What do we have that makes us worth belonging to? What, in other words, is our big idea?

CHAPTER FOUR

towards a big idea

Today, more than ever, the business world is full of ideas. Good and bad, fresh and stale, worthwhile and merely modish. Ideas for new business models, ideas for new products, ideas like 'focus' and other management catchphrases. And ideas that are, in effect, corporate ideologies – the 'company way'.

Many of them are valuable in their own way, but organizations are discovering that they don't do enough. They don't help differentiate organizations – they don't make them stand out in a noisy marketplace. They don't engage people. They don't nourish life.

Organizations are searching for something bigger.

More emotional than a business model

People often talk in excited tones about new 'business models'. What they normally mean is new ways of conducting a business, usually at considerably lower cost than before. A new business model may involve, for instance, a slicker manufacturing process, or a streamlined distribution channel.

Electronic commerce is currently creating dozens of new business models in this vein: the bookshop that has no shelves; the virtual travel agency; the electronic auctioneer;

the flight-booker where you name the fare you're prepared to pay.

Business models like these can be impressive generators of revenue (and, over time, profit). And they certainly count as ideas. But they're not the kind of big idea that this book is about.

They are simply ideas about a way of doing business, not about what that business stands for, for its employees and its customers.

A fashionable business model for banks and insurance companies is 'bancassurance' – the idea that a company can make more money by selling both banking and insurance products. This is the supreme example of a business model that's not a big idea, because it has no emotional resonance for customers or employees. Everyone suspects it's merely a way for big institutions to cut costs. There's a huge prize waiting to be claimed by the first company to turn bancassurance into its own unique big idea – into something that customers can't wait to buy, and employees can energetically buy into.

Because business models are simply about a way of doing business, they are eminently imitable. In the PC business, for instance, Dell has been admired for years for its business model: making PCs to customers' specifications, so that stock is kept to the barest minimum. But by 1998, Compaq and IBM, its two main rivals, were catching up. Since then, both Dell and Compaq have moved on again. Dell is now trying to move on from a business model to a bigger idea, through advertising in which Michael Dell himself asserts that Dell believes in 'being direct'.

And most traditional bookshops around the world are emulating the business model of Amazon. What they can't so easily copy is the experience of dealing with the company. What will make or break Amazon is its big idea – the idea of 'completeness' – not its business model.

Under the pressure of copycat competition, business models change over time. Orange started with a model that was about 'wirefree communication'. With the rise of the internet, they saw their model as 'the complete communication company'. It will no doubt change again. But their big idea won't.

The truth is that any good organization needs both: a clever business model, and a richly compelling big idea. The business model may well change completely over time: the big idea is much more stable. The business model guarantees some way of making money (even if it's in the distant future). The big idea engages people. Without a sturdy business model, the organization will run out of funding. And without a big idea, it will – sooner or later – run out of people. Consumers-with-attitude will spurn it. The best employees will go elsewhere. Investors will put their money into something more exciting.

There are other kinds of idea as well as business models. Product ideas, for example.

It's claimed that the US manufacturer Rubbermaid produces a new product every day. And behind every new product, and every new service, is an idea. But product ideas don't create long-term advantage. Competitors are quick to exploit good ideas. Procter & Gamble invented a new spray to eliminate smells in fabrics, and called it Febreze. Within a few months, Johnson & Johnson, Chlorox and others had launched their own versions.

A product idea is not the same thing as a big idea. The two are, of course, intimately connected. Good product ideas flow readily from a strong underlying organizational idea. Pret a Manger, the British sandwich shop chain part-owned by McDonald's, has an organizational idea that lunchtime food can be as stylish and enticing as fashionable clothes; and this idea has fuelled a steady succession of new sandwiches, non-sandwich products like sushi, and juices unique to the store. But the Pret a Manger idea is larger than any of its products: indeed, it could change its complete range of products (and probably has changed most of them over its lifetime), but still be Pret a Manger.

Organizations capable of long-lasting success do not depend on a particular product idea. Their organizational idea generates their product ideas, and not vice versa; and is big enough to generate an almost inexhaustible range of product ideas. For example, the organizational idea of 'making people happy' drove the creation of Disney as a company; and Disney became the kind of company that could make *Fantasia* and Disneyland and the city of Celebration and whatever new products it announces in the new century.

Of course, some product ideas are bigger than others. A mobile phone manufacturer might think 'let's make this black phone in pink plastic too': this could be a good and profitable idea, but it's a small and specific one. A larger idea would be 'let's make this mobile phone in a range of metallic colours'. Larger still would be an idea like 'let's do for mobile phones what Swatch did for watches'. The bigger the idea, the wider its implications: the more additional product ideas it suggests, the more fecund it is.

And there comes a stage at which an idea becomes too big to be simply a product idea, and starts to look much more like the organizational idea we're concerned with.

If our imaginary mobile phone maker decided 'let's make phones into a form of self-expression', they'd be on to something big.

Alongside product ideas, the business world is full of ideas on how to manage better.

For instance, almost every strategy expert over the last twenty years has preached *focus*. Peters and Waterman, back in the early 1980s, showed how what they called excellent companies 'stick to the knitting': they concentrate on what they're best at. Meanwhile, conglomerates went out of fashion as investors found direct use of the stockmarket a more efficient way of spreading an investment over a range of industries.

As a result, businesses worldwide have defined their core businesses, and divested everything that is not core. Hanson, once the world's most admired conglomerate, is now a building products company.

But focusing on a particular product segment, or a particular market sector, or a particular core competency, is not the same thing as having a big idea. This kind of focus is about *what* you choose to do, not *how* you do it: so, once again, it's imitable.

And it's perfectly possible to be relatively unfocused in the traditional sense, but nevertheless to run a purposeful business driven by a simple big idea.

Focus is one of the most seductive of management ideas, but it's far from the only one. Most organizations in the last decade have embraced ideas like re-engineering, total quality management, enterprise systems, empowerment and the learning organization.

All of these concepts are ideas. Many are ideas about how to do things. Some define what the experience of working for an organization should be like. But none is a big idea in our sense, simply because they're generic.

Indeed, there's a clear law of diminishing returns here. If you re-engineer, so can your rivals, and any advantage you've gained is quickly lost. In some industries, such as chemicals, almost every player has introduced an enterprise system – a comprehensive, company-wide computer system which demands that the company runs things its way.

As a result, organization structures, management methods and measurement techniques have become very similar across whole industries: in the end, no one has gained a competitive advantage.

The kind of big idea we're talking about has the opposite effect: it creates real and sustainable difference between an organization and its rivals.

More sensuous than ideology

All the ideas we've looked at so far – business models, product ideas, points of focus and gurus' catchphrases – are predominantly rational. Big ideas are much more emotional. They are much more about the spirit of an organization. And they are much more powerful at driving behaviour.

One way of describing an idea that influences behaviour is an ideology. The bestselling *Built to Last* looks at 18 of America's most admired companies – those seen as 'visionary' – and shows how important ideology has been for these visionary businesses. The book's conclusion is that 'the existence of a core ideology [is] a primary element in the historical development of visionary companies'.

The book goes on to define ideology as a combination of two things – core values and purpose. It argues that, in all these visionary companies, this core ideology is a constant, which is not allowed to change over time. Conversely, everything else – products, markets, organization structures, and so on – is allowed to change. Indeed, change is strongly and systematically encouraged. So a company is nothing other than its core values and purpose.

Ideologies served American companies well in the twentieth century. Hewlett-Packard, with its strong ethical principles, was one of the most admired twentieth-century companies. The department store Nordstrom, whose culture is said to be almost cult-like in its intensity, and where so-called 'Nordies' chant 'we're number one' at 7 am department meetings, has been hugely successful (though, interestingly, it hasn't expanded outside America). And Andersen Consulting (now Accenture), whose recruits go through a compulsory induction process at their Chicago training centre, and who are often known outside the company as 'androids', has grown by 20 per cent or more every year of its existence.

But, at least in their barest form, these ideologies will not be enough in the wider world, nor in this new century.

Ideology will not convince employees who feel increasingly free to move between companies, and who are increasingly sceptical about corporatism.

Ideology will not convince employees in the rest of the world who never have been as open to the myths American corporations tell themselves.

Ideology belongs to the old century, to the era of company man. Although people still want to belong, they're increasingly reluctant to sign up to an ideology.

And ideology will be irrelevant to consumers, who will be interested in a company's purpose and values only if they generate something special for customers.

In other words, both employees and consumers will demand something richer, something more experiential, something more emotional, something more *sensuous* than ideology.

Towards a big idea

The last three decades have seen organizations travel in search of that 'something more sensuous'. Their first calling point was corporate identity.

Corporate identity originated in the USA in the 1940s, but it wasn't until the 1970s that it joined the management lexicon. Gurus like Wally Olins preached the value of making your strategy visible through symbols, logotypes, colours and typefaces.

At the very least, these devices helped to make clear the relationships between component divisions in complex businesses: the rise of corporate identity coincided, interestingly, with the rise of the diversified corporation.

But the best corporate identity work went far beyond that, and brought a new quality of evocation, sometimes even of beauty, to corporate symbolism.

Most organizations, however, commissioned dreary and repetitive logos that said nothing about them and made little difference to their success. Travel through France and, as you pass from region to region, and from department to department, you're greeted by a gallery of welcome signs, each with a logo more banal than the last. Travel by train in Britain, and you're bewildered and disorientated by train company logos, almost all of them woefully unimaginative. Corporate identities like these, instead of raising their owners above the visual noise in their marketplace, simply add to it.

And the weakness they share is that they represent nothing: they are mere devices, with no idea behind them, with nothing to stand for. Indeed, some organizations who've undertaken corporate identity projects find that they've ended up with little more than a smart letterhead and need to start another exercise to find a personality to underlie the new logo.

More solid than vision

Corporate identity work, good and bad, has continued. However, in the 1980s many organizations became less concerned about their outward symbolism, and more concerned about their inward purpose. Senior management believed that, in a world where technology was creating increasingly rapid change, their employees needed to share a view of what the business was there to do. Writers like Tom Peters created a great deal of excitement about releasing the potential of employees, turning every company into an 'excellence' organization.

By the end of the decade, almost every organization, and every division within every organization, had a mission statement. Most included the word 'excellence': Tom Peters has been one of the most influential men in the corporate world.

But all these mission statements looked pretty much the

same. In fact, you can now get software that generates random mission statements by stringing together standard phrases from the impoverished vocabulary of 'mission'.

As well as being dishearteningly unoriginal, these mission statements were also largely ineffectual. They were displayed, nicely framed, in canteens and reception areas, but, as Eileen Shapiro suggested in her book, *Fad Surfing in the Boardroom*, most mission statements were little more than 'a talisman, hung in public places, to ward off evil spirits'.

Gradually, the mood changed. In business, and in politics too, a demand grew for what was called 'the vision thing'. Instead of mission statements, organizations created visions. The military analogy of 'mission' turned into the more spiritual analogy of 'vision'.

But the content changed less. Missions and visions both tended to be about one or more of three things. First, a statement of purpose: why the organization exists. Second, a statement of ambition: where the organization wants to get to. Third, a statement of values: what the organization believes in.

Some missions and visions were relatively precise. General Electric, for example, set out to 'become number one or number two in every market we serve and revolutionize this company to have the speed and agility of a small enterprise'. Compare this with Westinghouse's vaguer statement: 'Total quality, Market leadership, Technology driven, Global, Focused growth, Diversified.'

But both of these statements are like a million others around the world. They once made sense – indeed, they probably resonated deeply – on a flipchart at the end of a senior management retreat. But they're too bare, too generic, too abstract, to drive experience.

Most of the time, these statements are nothing but words. They're often highly abstract, and fail to guide people in their day-to-day behaviour. And they're rarely truthful: they do not correspond with the messy reality that employees see around them every day.

Most of these statements are the product of compromise. In the interests of involving people in their creation (a noble aspiration), they end up being designed by committee. From the often heated debates that result, what emerge are the coldest of lowest-common-denominators. Vision, which should be an act of leadership, becomes an act of fudge.

Just before it was bought by the Royal Bank of Scotland, the giant NatWest undertook one of these values exercises – no better and no worse than many others. Staff took part in workshops where they were asked to follow a series of five 'work mats', in order to learn about NatWest's six values. These values – customer focus, trust, teamwork, innovation, excellence and passion – could belong to absolutely anyone. One insider commented, 'I suppose we should have realized we were doomed at that point.' Whatever the justice of that, it's certainly true that the promulgation of bland sets of values does nothing to create a vigorous, differentiated organization.

And mission and vision have another weakness. They appeal only to an internal audience: the organization's employees, and in particular its managers. The simple ambition that drives Microsoft – Windows everywhere – is like this. It may excite insiders, but it offers customers nothing to buy into.

Deeper than brand

Through the 1990s, the pendulum swung back, away from the introspective missions and visions to something much more outward-directed, and much less abstract: brand.

A concept that had been applied for a century to consumer products began to be applied to whole organizations – even to complex ones like professional services firms which don't sell products and don't sell to consumers. By the end of the decade, a typical edition of *The Economist* might include expensive brand-building advertising for Accenture, Ernst & Young, KPMG and Pricewaterhouse-Coopers.

Manufacturers created consumer product brands to differentiate their products from goods sold in plain paper bags in groceries. The brand label said, in effect, 'You can see who made this product and therefore trust it to be reliable.' The brand, in other words, was much more than a label or a logo: it was a promise. The brand promised consumers that, every time they bought that product, they would get the same experience. Every bottle of Coca-Cola would taste exactly the same.

In return for this level of confidence, consumers would pay more: brands could command premium pricing. Consumers would also repeat-buy: brands could increase sales. And consumers would experiment with new products that carried the same brand – brand extensions. So brands could enable their owners to diversify.

These three prizes – premium pricing, increased sales, and safer diversification – started to look very attractive to companies that sold not products, but services – so a new kind of brand, the service brand, emerged. And some wanted to gain these benefits for their whole organization, through a corporate brand.

The problem is that if a brand is a promise, that promise must be kept. The experience must be identical for consumers, time after time. Through rigorous quality control, product companies can achieve that level of consistency. Every Kit Kat is the same.

But service companies depend on their people. And people aren't consistent. It's very hard for a service business like British Airways or Holiday Inn or Club Med to deliver complete consistency.

Some work towards it by making their service as much like a product as possible: for McDonald's, for instance, the food itself, and the design of the restaurants, is easily reproducible, and is made to form a much more important part of the consumer experience than the behaviour of its staff, which isn't so easily reproducible.

But the whole idea of brand hits its limits with businesses like professional services firms, where there's little scope to make the service more like a product. Indeed, some clients buy the very individuality of the partner they deal with – total consistency is not what they want.

By the end of the decade, the idea of brand, in its original form, started to look inadequate. It over-promised to consumers, and in some cases suggested a kind of uniformity that they didn't want. Worse, by speaking directly to consumers, it didn't speak to the needs and concerns of employees, the very people who were meant to keep the brand promise.

Many organizations felt themselves to be in a different world from consumer goods – professional firms, public agencies and charities for example – and their employees were deeply mistrustful of the idea of brand, thinking of it as a mere sugar-coating.

So what organizations started to look for was something deeper than brand. Something that, unlike product idea or business model, would be rich and sensuous. And something that, unlike vision or brand, would appeal to people inside and outside the organization equally: something they could share.

Big ideas

We've already found that vision is too inward-looking, and brand too outward-looking. What kind of idea can appeal to every stakeholder?

The idea must, in a sense, come before brand. In other words, it must drive the kind of promise that the organization makes.

Howard Schultz was once asked by *USA Today* how he created Starbucks as a huge brand. His response was that he didn't set out to create a brand – he set out to create a really good company, and the brand developed.

In other words, get the big idea right, and its external manifestation, the brand, will to a large extent take care of itself.

A big idea that can create or nourish a really good company must probably do four things, for both outsiders and insiders.

First, it must make the organization valuable. The organization must meet people's real needs – tomorrow's as well as today's, and emotional as well as practical.

Second, it must make the organization different – the organization must offer something unique. This is essential if customers are going to buy from it – and if employees are going to work for it.

Third, it must bind people together, creating a sense of belonging for employees *and* customers.

Fourth, it must celebrate people's differences. A big idea creates unity, but never uniformity. This is clearly true of employees, but it's also true of the effect the organization has on its customers. As employees, we're knowledge workers, valuing our independence of thought – something customers want too. A monolithic brand – remorselessly creating identical experiences – is undesirable as well as impossible.

All of this adds up to something you could call 'unity of feeling'. Go back a century and consider the Rothschilds, the first international financial services company, with businesses in London, Paris, Frankfurt, Vienna and Naples.

The prosperity of the Rothschilds, wrote Disraeli, a close friend of the family, 'was as much owing to the unity of feeling which pervaded all branches of that numerous family as in their capital and abilities'.

What drove the success of the Rothschilds, then, was not their 'core competencies', their business model or their market insight. Nor was it their corporate identity, their vision or their brand (they didn't have any of these things, in the modern sense of the words). It was the unity of feeling they created.

As well as going wide – inside and outside the organization – big ideas reach deeply within people.

Big ideas create a special kind of engagement with the organization: they lead people to identify with it. That's to say, people recognize an aspect of themselves in the organization, and so make the organization part of themselves.

How does it happen? You encounter an organization for the first time, and see something you like: something valuable, something different. The approval of friends often helps here: this is very much a social, rather than an individual, process. You start to interact with it, maybe buy something, maybe even take a job there. You start to feel a sense of belonging, but also a stronger sense of your own individuality. Your link with that organization then becomes part of your definition of yourself. Indeed, it expands and enriches your sense of yourself. Criticism of the organization feels like criticism of you. If the organization fails in some way, you feel wounded.

That's what an organization like Starbucks can do. At Starbucks, people don't just buy coffee, they engage with the whole Starbucks idea. At Mandarin Oriental hotels, people don't just stay the night, they feel part of a club. Customers and employees of Orange are 'Orange people'.

Creating this depth of engagement means appealing to people at many levels other than the purely rational. As we saw with the Rothschilds, this is a unity of feeling, not a unity of thought.

This intimacy is far more effective for organizations than vision or brand. People become much more than customers or employees: they become participators, creators and advocates.

A new way of business

What's emerging from all this isn't just big ideas: it's a new kind of corporation. 'There's a new way of running a business,' says Orange's Hans Snook. 'It's based on integrity, on believing what you say, and on attempting to deliver on it.'

So how is this new way of running a business different?

Old organizations claim to be 'customer-driven'. The new organization stands for something. It *proposes* something which customers then engage with – it doesn't wait for customers to tell it what to do. Big idea companies gain stature by refusing to pander to customer demands, where those demands would undermine the big idea.

Old organizations aimed to win the loyalty of their customers and employees. The new organization goes beyond loyalty. Someone once said, sadly, 'loyalty is what remains when belief has gone'. Companies with a big idea inspire belief: something more intelligent, more deeply motivating, more dynamic, something that can make them want to change the way they behave.

Old organizations – those that are commercial at any rate – aim for profit, or maybe for long-term shareholder value. The new organization aims for a goal beyond profit, which can inspire all its stakeholders.

Old organizations use 'vision' and 'brand' as tools. New organizations see their big idea not as a *tool* but as their *core*. They exist to make their big idea a reality, and so – in one way or another – to nourish life.

And that's just what we're now starting to see in the world's marketplace.

A simple example is Nike, which makes sports shoes, but which stands for the bigger idea of 'winning'. Its soul is about winning.

Another is Amazon, which on the surface sells books (and other things), but is actually about 'completeness' – the idea that anybody can get anything. That's why the arrow on its logo goes from the 'a' to the 'z' of 'amazon'. Indeed, its founder, Jeff Bezos, has said that anyone who thinks that Amazon is in the bookselling business has no idea what Amazon's game plan is.

Or IKEA, which makes furnishings, but stands for the bigger idea of 'a better everyday life for the many'.

Or the BBC, a broadcaster, which stands for the bigger idea of 'authoritativeness'. It provides authoritative news and information, and sets an authoritative standard in entertainment.

Or Starbucks, which is about 'sociability' more than it's about coffee – about providing a place where people feel at home as they drink coffee, chat or read the papers.

Or Cisco, a manufacturer of equipment for electronic networks, which believes in an 'outside in' way of running a business, where customers have an unusual degree of power over the organization's strategy.

Or Southwest, the airline that lives and breathes a spirit of 'irreverence' – where flying is fun.

Or Muji, the retailer of homewares and clothing, which believes in simple designs and natural materials, rather than the flashiness of many branded goods.

This phenomenon isn't restricted to fashionable, highly brand-conscious companies. It applies to workaday businesses like insurance, air cargo, distribution, building products, water utilities, outsourcing companies, paper manufacturers and law firms. Though there may be only one or two companies with a big idea in these areas now, in a few years there will be dozens.

And like all ideas, these organizational big ideas are most potent when they resonate with larger social changes. As the American magazine the *Nation* famously wrote in 1943, 'There is one thing stronger than all the armies in the world, and that is an idea whose time has come.' Muji's idea of plainness resonates with a wider desire for the authentic. IKEA's democratization of design coincides with a wider drive to remove barriers of class and wealth.

Idea versus idea

This is an extraordinary, and relatively new, development.

It means that the landscape is changing. Instead of an array of organizations, large and small, doing a million different things, the world of work is changing into a world of ideas. Ideas are starting to matter more than the organizations that embody them.

Instead of Apple versus Microsoft, British Airways versus Virgin, Sony versus Bang & Olufsen, we're moving to a new set of battles. Apple stands for difference, Microsoft for ubiquity: which do you identify with? British Airways offers a kind of reassurance, Virgin a more youthful iconoclasm: which idea can capture more passengers? Sony is about perfectionism, Bang & Olufsen about poetry: which is the bigger idea in the new century?

People are responding to, and engaging with, the ideas that seem right to them, or right for them.

In a way, the emergence of idea-led organizations isn't

so surprising. Not when consumers are crying out for organizations to stand for something. Not when investors want organizations to own a magic wellspring of future value. Not when people want to work for organizations that share their own values and priorities.

And when all these groups of people overlap, it's not so surprising that organizations are looking for *one* thing to say to all of them. Or, to put it more grandly, that organizations are searching for a way to create the sort of 'unity of feeling' that drove the success of that early global firm, Rothschilds.

In a world of over-communication – in a marketplace that's far too noisy – a few organizations are finding bigger, simpler ideas that enable them to rise above the din.

CHAPTER FIVE

the soul of the organization

A big idea is the soul of an organization. It's not a form of words: it's the organization's essence.

Tesco, the British supermarket group, has a stated vision 'to create value for customers to earn their lifetime loyalty'. Its brand is built around the phrase 'every little helps'. But anyone who has ever encountered the company knows that Tesco is about much more.

Tesco's big idea – palpable in (almost) every store – is richer, more multi-dimensional than either of those statements. It's about the relationship between the company and its customers, about the look and even the smell of the stores, it's about how the checkout person greets you, it's about Tesco's stand against genetically modified ingredients, it's about Tesco's aggressive growth, it's about how Tesco makes you feel.

In a phrase, Tesco's big idea is 'we like our customers'.

This extra substance and extra depth are what make big ideas so fascinating. Investigating them means touching something powerful, yet also elusive. Something that's not an artificial construct, but the truth about the organization. Something that's recognizable by everyone who encounters the organization, and that excites and engages many of those people.

As the writer and broadcaster Charles Handy says, soul is:

one of those concepts that, like beauty, evaporates when you try to define it, but like beauty it is instantly recognizable when you meet it. Organizations have a feel about them, a feel which the visitor picks up as soon as he or she enters the building or, often, merely encounters the people who work there. . . . There is a sense that the organization is on some sort of crusade, not just to make money, but something grander, something worthy of one's commitment, time and skills.

That's why big ideas are so powerful. It's also why big ideas are very hard to define: they're never adequately captured by a glib word or phrase.

Strictly speaking – legally and theologically – corporations don't have souls. The seventeenth-century jurist Sir Edward Coke declared that corporations 'cannot commit treason, nor be outlawed nor excommunicated, for they have no souls'.

But plenty of people these days see it differently. Julian Metcalfe, for instance, founder of the sandwich shop chain Pret a Manger, believes passionately that 'a company has a soul'. An admirer of enlightened Quaker businesses like Cadbury, he's fired by more complex aims than making money. Indeed, he claims 'I never look at the figures, ever. The idea that the pursuit of profit is everything – it's criminal.'

This soul may be sensuous, or emotional, or ethical, or even spiritual – or, most likely of all, a mix of those things. For instance, the big idea behind Mandarin Oriental hotels, 'moments of pleasure', is at least partly sensuous: it's about creating a curtain of mystique and then quickly letting people in through the curtain.

The big ideas behind Orange ('optimism') and Disney ('fun') are emotional. The big ideas behind John Lewis Partnership ('a better form of capitalism') and Amnesty International ('human rights') are ethical or even political. The big idea behind hi-fi company Bang & Olufsen (creating a kind of 'poetry') is almost spiritual. So is the big idea behind the National Trust (the idea that places of historic interest or natural beauty have a special 'spirit of the place' that's worth protecting for everyone to enjoy).

But these big ideas aren't just wishy-washy feelings. They are points of view. They are *for* some things and *against* others. The BBC is for authoritative and against exploitative broadcasting. The airline Go is for equality and against deference. The huge Indian conglomerate Tata is for fair play and against corruption.

But how do you capture a soul? How can you put it into words? A big idea is complex, not neat and tame, and its wildness is the source of much of its power. Defining it may make it manageable: but it may also diminish that profusion, or even make it no longer visible. 'Definition', as Samuel Butler wrote, 'is the enclosing a wilderness of idea within a wall of words.'

Many organizations with big ideas have tried to build just such a wall of words. Some have done this for internal reasons, because they feel they ought to have a 'vision' they can communicate to staff. But of course big ideas go beyond the internal, and almost all attempts at definition fall short of capturing the real thing.

For most organizations, there's a huge gulf between the official vision and the real big idea, the real soul.

For example, the Australian wine producer Southcorp has an official vision that's about being international, summed up as 'wines and the world'. But Southcorp's big idea is bigger than that: it's about a different attitude to winemaking. It's about using different techniques to beat the best in the world.

Southcorp's most famous wine is Grange, produced since the 1950s (a 1955 bottle can cost $14,000), and the American wine critic Robert Parker has written that Grange 'has replaced Bordeaux's Pétrus as the world's most exotic and concentrated wine'. This kind of achievement exemplifies the big idea behind Penfolds, and Bruce Kemp, the man behind Southcorp, reveals his true passion – the real soul of Southcorp – when he talks about Grange. 'It's right up there with the French first growth wines,' he says, 'but it's not from one vineyard or even one region.' Southcorp can produce great wine without any of the old-world hang-ups.

Official statements of vision, mission, values or whatever always seem to be inadequate. Some are better than others, but – going back to Samuel Butler's metaphor – they always feel more like the wall than the wilderness. 'Wines and the world' can't begin to capture the spirit of Southcorp, its self-belief, its inventiveness, its Australian-ness even, let alone the rich wine-drinking experiences it makes for its customers. 'Lifetime customer loyalty' is a useful shorthand, but it's easy to say, and dozens of lesser companies than Tesco have said it. It points to some of the things that are special about Tesco, but falls a long way short of expressing them.

What, then, are these curiously elusive big ideas like? Can the wilderness be described, if not tamed? For all their rich variety, what do big ideas have in common?

Changing the world

The first common characteristic of big ideas is that they're radical. Jeff Bezos of Amazon has famously said, 'our model is work hard, have fun, make history'.

There are two ways to deal with the world: adapt yourself to it, or change it. Big ideas want to change the world.

Big ideas react against the status quo. Big ideas go to the root of the matter, rather than just pruning its branches. Big ideas are nonconformist: they go against the grain of conventional thinking.

Sometimes, it's not so much a big idea, more a big *ideal*.

'I may be a businessman,' says Sir Richard Branson, 'in that I set up and run companies for profit, but when I try to plan ahead and dream up new products and new companies I'm an idealist.'

Most organizations start with a big ideal – even if over time it gets forgotten or compromised or confused. The impulse that creates an organization – that overcomes all the inertia, that wins over the founding investors, that battles against the early setbacks – has got to be something powerful, something big, something that touches people deeply. Starting an organization, says Apple's Steve Jobs, is 'so hard that if you don't have a passion, you'll give up. There were times in the first two years when we could have given up and sold Apple, and it probably would've died.'

It's not always explicit, but every organization starts by wanting to make a difference of some kind.

Ross Perot, the former US presidential candidate, was an IBM salesman until he decided to create EDS, one of the world's first computer services companies. He found a new way of looking at computers – not as a product, but as the means of providing a service. And now of course most computer companies, IBM included, make far more money from selling services than from selling computers.

But that, interestingly, wasn't the big idea. That was the business model, not the driving impulse. The driving impulse, so the story goes, came from a quotation Perot saw in *Reader's Digest*, from Thoreau's book of essays, *Walden*: 'The mass of men lead lives of quiet desperation.' This was what Perot wanted to change: he didn't want the mechanized life of an IBM product salesman. (The EDS he created turned out to be uncannily similar to IBM in the end – with its insistence on dark suits and white shirts – but that's another story.)

That same Thoreau quotation resonates deeply for another, more recent, entrepreneur, Hans Snook at Orange. 'Most people want more freedom,' he says. 'Most men lead lives of quiet desperation.' So how did that thought turn into Orange, with its big idea of 'optimism'?

'I didn't start out to create a big idea,' Hans Snook insists. 'I find it incredibly hard to talk about it. But part of it is the desire to do something better, creating a better world, creating a new condition. Everyone has this creative well-spring. If you create an environment that allows people to be more creative, to do things better, that leads to optimism.' For Hans Snook, it's this kind of deeper impulse that drove the creation of Orange, and that the organization still lives by. 'It's a virtuous circle,' he says. 'Freedom leads to creativity leads to a better world leads to optimism leads to more freedom.'

Or, as Orange's launch advertising put it: 'don't worry, the future's bright, the future's Orange'.

Ross Perot and Hans Snook, both of them partly impelled by that bleak line from Thoreau, each started a business, and changed their industry. Of course, as Hans Snook says, Thoreau's thought is a very general one, and the desire to reduce the world's quiet desperation could lead to all sorts of organizations. 'This virtuous circle idea', he says, 'could apply to any business. It's how you particularize it that matters.'

This kind of nonconformist thinking isn't new. In the nineteenth century, many of Britain's most successful businesspeople were Quakers – literally nonconformist. They created companies like Barclays in banking, Rowntree and Cadbury in chocolate, and Clarks in shoes. In a turbulent and unprincipled marketplace, they succeeded in making better products and in creating better working conditions. They anticipated the idea of the organization as community by a hundred years: Rowntree's *Cocoa Works Magazine* hoped in 1902 that 'in combining social progress with commercial success, the entire body of workers must be animated with a common aim'.

Do all organizations start with a desire to escape from 'quiet desperation'? Of course not. Most start with 'wouldn't it be fun if . . .' or 'someone should do something about this . . .' or 'if we pool our skills, we could make some money'. Even the Quakers were driven by commercial as much as by philanthropic aims. But underlying those thoughts are deeper convictions about what counts as fun, what matters, what's worthwhile. In a small or a big way, most organizations start off by wanting to change things.

And it's those deeper convictions that most organizations forget, or fail to live by. If more organizations could rediscover their founding convictions – and make them relevant to tomorrow's world – they'd achieve their explicit aims more easily. They would make more money, raise more funding, attract better staff, stand out more clearly in the marketplace.

There are many ways of being radical. Some organizations reinvent their particular product or market: their radical question is 'how could our market be better?' Others pioneer better ways of running a business: their radical question is 'how could business be better?' Still others want to inspire people to feel or act differently, and their radical question is 'how could the world be better?'

Hi-fi company Bang & Olufsen challenges the way consumer electronic products tend to be, and rethinks them. 'We turn technology into concept,' says former chief executive Anders Knutsen. 'For example, we introduced widescreen television three years after everyone else, but as a home cinema system, incorporating video. We clean up the mess that others leave behind. We reinvent hi-fi by giving it another expression.'

Similarly, Saturn set out to change everything about selling cars. 'We knew from the beginning', says Saturn dealer Stuart Lasser, 'that if Saturn was to succeed, we'd have to do more than just sell a good car. We'd also have to change the way cars are sold, the way people who sell them are perceived, and the way customers feel about the experience of shopping for a car.'

'Saturn stepped into a void,' agrees Nancy Brown Johnson, the company's director of organizational development. 'The whole industry was not very customer-focused. It was an adversarial environment. No one wanted to partner with customers. Our tag line is "a different kind of company", but we were not different just to be cute. Something had to change.'

Japanese retailer Muji set out to change the way people buy high-fashion items like clothes and furniture. Its idea was to provide inexpensive simple, basic products, with no designer labels, around which people could build their own lifestyles. 'The main idea', says Ariga Kaoru, 'is that consumers can combine things among our products, clothes, homewares. As a result, our colours are muted, our designs aren't edgy.'

That's the pragmatic bit: but Muji has an idealistic dimension too. 'Our idea has a logical, practical basis, but at the same time it's very important to hold on to the things we really believe in. For example, we want to be able to provide products that are close to their natural state, with as few artificial processes behind them as possible.' Plainness and naturalness are part of the soul of Muji. But so is individuality – for the business, as well as for customers. Though Muji plans to grow, growth is not Ariga Kaoru's primary aim. 'We have never said that to sell more is better – that's not our motivation at all. Our motivation is "to have individuality". Our main driving force is finding ways to provide products and develop our stores in a way that no other company has achieved before.'

Apple set out to change the way people use computers, and, more importantly, the way they feel about computers. This radical thinking deeply influences the way they design their products. The sleep light on the Apple iBook, for instance, doesn't blink on and off, like ordinary computers. A blinking light, as the iBook's designer, Jonathan Ive, says, 'solves the functional problem, which is to describe a state the object is in'. But that's not how Apple sees things. 'We felt the blinking light did it in a machine-like way. For the iBook, we developed a sleep light that glows on and off. When people describe it, they say that it looks like the computer is breathing or beating . . . That light illustrates the difference we're seeking to make in the industry.'

Starbucks overturned the way people think about coffee, from commodity to sophisticated pleasure, from something to grab when you've a moment to something to devote time to. It all seems so natural now, that it's hard to remember how radical a change this is.

Charles Schwab changed the way people buy and sell shares – not just through its business model (discount brokerage) but through a revolutionary attitude ('the customer is smart'). This attitude was daringly new in financial services – natural though it seems to us now.

HSBC is just starting to change the way people think about banks – from national or local institutions to a single worldwide service company – though it's too early to say yet whether the transformation is succeeding.

But big ideas can aim to change more than just the nature of a particular product. Some try to change the nature of business itself, or at least to demonstrate a better way of doing business.

The John Lewis Partnership was created with a hugely radical big idea – 'a better form of capitalism' – soon after the Russian Revolution. The company is owned by its employees, and has developed a way of doing business that aims to be non-adversarial. Customers know that if they have a problem, the store will sort it out: rarely if ever will they have to fight. Staff defuse customers' problems not by apologizing but by *sympathizing*: if a customer brings back a teapot with a broken handle, for instance, the china assistant says, 'How awful, you didn't burn yourself did you?', and instantly organizes a replacement. The angry shopper becomes a friend: what could have been confrontation becomes congeniality.

And finally, the American financial services company Fannie Mae – now one of the country's largest – has been built on the radical purpose of democratizing home-ownership. By 1998, Fannie Mae was halfway to its $1 trillion commitment to provide targeted lending to ten million low and moderate income families.

Some big ideas go even further, and aim to touch and change people deeply.

Go's Barbara Cassani has a simple view of the world: 'I hate deference.' She created Go in reaction to the elaborate caste systems of other airlines, where the quality of your experience depends on whether you can afford business class or maybe even, holy of holies, first class. 'We make no assumption that customers are rich or poor,' she says: 'everyone can find a home with us.' By reacting against something she didn't like, Barbara Cassani has changed the world – she's created a low-cost airline that doesn't offer cheapness but 'equality', a classless airline that makes budget travellers feel good about themselves.

Even something as workaday as a business park can aspire in this direction. Chiswick Park in west London, designed by Richard Rogers, aims to do more than provide an efficient office environment. It believes in 'the right to enjoy work'. It has established a wide range of services to minimize frustration and maximize stimulation. People there will do your shopping for you, or track down the resources you need, or arrange art shows at lunchtime, or even give everyone a doughnut as they arrive in the morning. Everything's designed to help people enjoy work more.

Simpler still, and huge in its impact, is the big idea behind Disney. 'We sell fun,' says chief executive Michael Eisner. 'And – not to sound arrogant, really just to sound proud – we still do that better than anyone.' One of the biggest of all big ideas, this thought now drives not just the original Disney animation business and its four theme parks, but also three other film studios, two cruise ships, 725 Disney stores, ABC television, and the sports cable network ESPN. In Anaheim they're building Disney's California Adventure, and DisneySea is taking shape in Tokyo. The great power of Disney is not just to produce fun (and all of it in a carefully policed 'good taste'), but to produce fun across all of these different businesses. The same Disney character can star in an animated film, a theme-park ride, toys in the Disney stores, records, maybe even a musical – and it all gets reported in Disney's magazines and on the Disney television channels worldwide.

Like Go, IKEA has a democratic founding impulse. 'Most of the time', its founder Ingvar Kamprad affirms, 'beautifully designed home furnishings are created for a small part of the population – the few who can afford them. From the beginning, IKEA has taken a different path. We have decided to side with the many.'

Everyone's property

A big idea may start with a radical impulse in one person's mind, but in the end it belongs to customers, employees, investors, the media – all the organization's stakeholders. It's everyone's property, and no one's. A big idea that never gets outside the founder's head is not a big idea. The second common characteristic of big ideas, therefore, is that they're social. IKEA's big idea doesn't belong to Ingvar Kamprad, but to all the people around the world who know IKEA. Big ideas are the focal point of a unity of feeling.

Guardian readers and *Guardian* writers, for instance, share a clear sense of what the *Guardian* stands for – it's about the responsibilities and pleasures of being an outsider. They may disagree about all sorts of things, but they share a unity of feeling. The idea belongs neither to the readers nor to the newspaper.

In America, Saturn was created to build a new spirit of harmony between a car company and the trade unions. But now the idea is much more widely owned. Saturn car owners feel part of something different, important and exciting – exciting enough to draw tens of thousands of them to the company's 'Homecoming' weekend at Spring Hill, Tennessee. 'We're amazed', say the company, 'that so many people would be willing to give up part of their summer vacations and drive hundreds, even thousands of miles to visit a place they only know about because they bought a car.' But that's the power of a socially owned big idea.

Equally, many Ben & Jerry's customers feel as much ownership of the company's big idea as Ben Cohen and Jerry Greenfield themselves, and amid rumours of an imminent takeover put their own time and money into campaigning to preserve 'their' organization's independence. The takeover went ahead – and a large part of what Unilever bought was this huge, intangible social property, the shared Ben & Jerry's idea.

These days everyone has a view about most of the world's best known organizations, and what (if anything) they stand for. Their big ideas, if they have one, are common property. These shared themes may be true or untrue, fair or unfair, but they are the force that, probably more than any other single force, will influence the future success of these organizations. And some of these big ideas are more compelling – are more likely to create future success – than others.

Big ideas are shared by employees too, of course, and are constantly being reinterpreted by them. Even an organization with a clear purpose like the National Trust faces this problem: Martin Drury says wryly that 'people are very ready to interpret our purpose in their own terms'.

Even so, there are usually strong shared themes, even in a complex organization like Shell – though these themes may be expressed in rather vague, tentative terms. 'We asked our people what Shell is about,' says chairman Sir Mark Moody-Stuart. 'Through eighty different sessions, the same elements came out. First, there was a feeling that Shell is intuitively international – many international idealists fetch up at Shell. Second, a shared sense of doing something useful, worthwhile, not trivial: we provide energy. And finally, a feeling of development – many of our people come from or work in developing economies.' Vague maybe, but widely shared.

There are few things more powerful than a socially shared idea, because it has a self-propelling energy to it. Economists like Paul Ormerod, in his book *Butterfly Economics*, are starting to recognize how buying decisions are made not individually but by collective influence. There's safety in numbers: the more people you see around you who believe that Coca-Cola is a friend to young people, the safer it feels to believe it yourself. Indeed, the harder it becomes to dissent. This phenomenon can lead to huge success – like the rise of the internet. Or, if the belief turns out to be ill-founded, it leads to equally huge disaster – as the victims of tulipomania in seventeenth-century Holland, or the South Sea Bubble in eighteenth-century England, found. At its worst, of course, it becomes the hysteria of the mob.

The social ownership of big ideas has two consequences.

First, a frightening thought: your big idea is not under your control. No organization owns the contents of its people's minds. Consumers judge Gap, Marks & Spencer and the rest by what they see, not by what those organizations say about themselves. The most any organization can do, in the end, is to find a big idea that resonates with the times, and then – most importantly of all – live up to it.

Second, a disconcerting thought: there's no final, correct way of expressing your big idea. Because it's in so many people's heads, it's constantly shifting, even if only very slightly. In Britain, a non-profit organization called the Soil Association acts as the accreditor of organically-produced food. Its big idea is about the virtues of organic farming. And yet there's much more to its attitude – to the way it does things, day by day. Director Patrick Holden says, 'We have a half minute of silence at the start of our Council meetings – I'm not quite sure why. But that's typical of organizations with big ideas. It's like rural folk knowledge. It can't be written down, it has to be passed down. You can't understand an attitude by reading about it.'

Orange keeps trying to write down its big idea. It has three different (though overlapping) sets of values: brand values, advertising values and organizational values. It has a philosophy, 'to make the world a better place'. People sometimes use the phrase 'a bright human future'. But in some ways, the most successful encapsulation of the big idea has been not words but an image – a seven-year-old child leading an adult by the hand. That picture says more than any words could about leading people away from 'quiet desperation'.

Made with actions

Big ideas are better expressed through what's done than what's said. The third common characteristic of big ideas is that they're visible – tangible, even – through the actions they inspire.

The French poet Mallarmé observed that poetry is written with words, not with ideas. In the same way, organizations are made with actions, not with ideas. They're made with products and services, not visions and values; and a big idea should be judged by actions, not words.

In organizations with big ideas, people do things because they want to, not because they've been trained by rote. There's a world of difference between the rather stilted, automatic Ritz-Carlton pause, and the way that staff in, for example, John Lewis stores naturally put themselves on your side. If you're looking for, say, a mushroom and garlic pizza in one of their Waitrose supermarkets, a staff member (no matter how junior) will take you to the right shelf, and if the shelf is empty will get a pizza from the storeroom and bring it to you, while you continue your shopping. And what matters is not that it's done, but that somehow it's done naturally and willingly.

And there's another world of difference between

management-speak and natural behaviour. Most companies talk rather artificially about the importance of teamwork. At Nike it's different. Founder Phil Knight says, 'The world of sports marks the way we talk to each other and how we relate. It's not like the imagined sports team in typical company parlance, but like the real team. Anyone can step up and make the play.'

In these ways, and many others, big ideas are tangible in organizations. They're not high-flown abstractions.

This is particularly clear when you talk to people who start up successful organizations. They're very matter-of-fact about what they do. Barbara Cassani, who set up the low-cost airline Go, says: 'All we can do is keep prices low, so that Go makes sense to people, and then give them a better experience, so that Go feels good.' Julian Metcalfe of Pret a Manger adopts a similar tone: 'We only sell fuel, it's very mundane. We simply do what we do, and do it beautifully, for both customers and staff, fifty-fifty.'

Simplicity is important. As Barbara Cassani says, 'None of this is brain surgery. We're just trying to do it in a very simple way. It's important not to take this too seriously: this is a business, not a religion.' This is, of course, much harder for bigger, older organizations. There the real challenge is to keep things simple: to rediscover the soul without getting religion.

So big ideas aren't fluffy. They're not religion. The proof of a big idea is in doing it, simply and consistently. And what that takes is steel – strength, determination, even maybe ruthlessness. Talking to people in organizations with big ideas, that steel is palpable.

Luckily, big ideas at their best give organizations a kind

of steel, a kind of toughness, a kind of structure. Big ideas create backbone because they're demanding.

IKEA's Ingvar Kamprad, for instance, has written that 'part of creating a better life for the many people also consists of breaking free from status and convention – becoming freer as human beings. We must, however, always bear in mind that freedom implies responsibility, meaning that we must demand much of ourselves.'

Big ideas are often about how things *ought to be*, and that sense of 'ought' sets a highly demanding standard – for both employees to achieve, and customers to monitor. This attitude can be an immensely effective way of running a company, because it challenges every employee to live up to their own sense of how things ought to be. It doesn't impose a standard. It doesn't expect a certain behaviour to be carried out by rote. Instead, it gets right inside every employee's own conscience.

Again, this doesn't need to be high-minded. Even an activity as mundane as delivering mail can be infused with this sense of 'ought'. The Swiss Post Office, for example, believes simply that the post is important, that getting it right is worthwhile. Every employee you encounter does things quietly the way they ought to be done.

Organizations with big ideas are often therefore a hard place to work. 'Tesco is a very hard, demanding place,' admits its chief executive, Terry Leahy. 'Any extraordinary performance, in music, sport or whatever, requires extraordinary behaviour, which can be quite chilling when taken out of context – but people will move heaven and earth if they think that what they're doing is recognized.' Big ideas, at their best, lead to extraordinary behaviour – because they create a climate that demands extraordinary behaviour.

That climate may not be explicit, may not be fully understood by everyone, but it's palpable. And you can see the results among Tesco executives. Patrick Holden from the Soil Association spoke about organic produce to a group of Tesco buyers, and found them 'lean, hungry, driven – driven in fact by something they didn't quite understand'.

Similarly life is tough at Go. 'If you don't want to work in a demanding environment', declares Barbara Cassani, 'you don't want to work for me.' And film industry analyst Robert Bucksbaum asks: 'Have you ever heard of any executive who's happy working with Michael Eisner?'

Though big ideas are often idealistic – about making the world a better place – they're commercial too. In America, Fannie Mae has one of the biggest of big ideas among financial companies – it provides home loans for minorities who've found them hard to get. The company says, 'Bringing business to minorities is morally right. It is also a business on which we make an attractive rate of return.'

Tesco, too, is resolutely commercial. Though its big idea is mainly about creating lifetime customer loyalty, there's another side to that coin. 'We've got a phrase in the business,' says Terry Leahy, 'follow the money.' What that means is that Tesco goes, almost by instinct, wherever people want to spend money. 'People's money isn't going into food any more, it's life, education, communication.' So Tesco is able swiftly to move into, for example, mobile phones. This is the commercial steel deep inside Tesco's big idea. But Terry Leahy recognizes that the rest of the big idea can't be forgotten. 'In financial services, mobile phones or whatever else we go into, we have to be able to demonstrate our values.'

Big ideas, then, are demanding. They create a climate that's tough and, often, very commercial. One of the strongest feelings among the chief executives I talked to was a sense – perhaps surprising – of chronic dissatisfaction. For them, nothing is ever quite good enough. It could always be better.

'We have more to do,' says Fannie Mae's Jim Johnson. 'We will not be satisfied until we are recognized as a world-class model of diversity.'

'The key is attention to detail,' says Alun Thomas, who runs Britain's Heathrow Express, recognized as a model transport service. 'There's always more you can do.'

Julian Metcalfe of Pret a Manger doodles restlessly on a paper napkin: 'We all have to drive ourselves – we could be ten times better.'

First Direct's attitude, which it shares with many of its customers, is frustration with the way banking used to be done. There has to be a better way. And still Andrew Armishaw is dissatisfied. 'I want more pace on some of the things we're doing,' he says. 'I'm impatient.'

Big ideas are tangible, but they're never completely realized. The organization never quite lives up to its big idea. It's that gap – that chronic dissatisfaction – that makes a big idea such a powerful, and relentless, driver of performance. That's why a big idea can charge up an organization, and keep it charged.

Soul-searching

A big idea is an organization's soul. It's intangible, immaterial, spiritual. But that doesn't mean it's inert. Quite the reverse. The Latin for soul is *anima*, and an organization's soul is the very thing that *animates* it.

We can all think of examples of soulless organizations: they seem to have no personality, no warmth, no colour, no spark, no energy. They do what they do, but they don't seem to *care* about it. They may even be soul-destroying – either to work for, or to buy from.

But most organizations do have a soul, somewhere. Many – perhaps most – don't yet understand it, aren't in touch with it. But it's there.

Finding that soul – understanding what the organization is really about – can be a hugely energizing experience. Articulating the deepest things it believes in is exciting and liberating. It excites the organization to do even better the things it does best. And it liberates it from doggedly pursuing what it never really believed in.

But finding a soul – a big idea – isn't easy.

It's not something you can make up. It's not a confection. It can't be wishful thinking. It must be the deepest truth about you. You can't *make* a big idea, you can only *find* it.

The secret is to look wide enough and deep enough, and to understand the full significance of what you discover: which means thought, reflection, contemplation.

It's emphatically not the traditional kind of corporate navel-gazing. It's not committees writing mission statements. It's not human resources people writing a list of the values they would like staff to believe in. It's not analysis-paralysis – putting everything on hold till 'the vision' is clear.

It's getting on with life, but reflecting on what you do, as you do it. And reflecting in a restless, demanding way that's never satisfied with glib answers. It means looking at achievements more than failures, and never getting discouraged or giving up. It means seeking others' views, and getting independent perspectives: outsiders can often see what's special about an organization more clearly than insiders. It means looking hard at what the organization actually does, and always asking why? and why? and why? And maybe never reaching the final answer.

In the very best sense of the word, it's soul-searching.

CHAPTER SIX

starting the journey

A big idea is its organization's soul. It's not something that can be conjured out of nothing: it's not a confection. Big ideas are found, not made.

So how do organizations find their big ideas?

Do they plan a great search, or stumble across the answer? Do they look deep into themselves, or scan the outside world? Do they dig up their pasts, or imagine their futures?

Is it a solitary pursuit, or a collective trek? Does it take sixty minutes, or sixty years? Is it a revelation, or a pilgrimage?

The answer is, in every case, both.

Finding a big idea is a strange, contradictory task, not a neat, step-by-step process. There is no formula, no recipe. A big idea is an organization's soul, and a soul is a hard thing to pin down or describe. Big ideas are social things – they live inside the minds of people inside and outside the organization – so they're hard to encapsulate. And organizations change constantly over time, so any kind of snapshot is limited and may be misleading.

The journey is complex because big ideas are themselves paradoxical. They are an inner conviction about the outer world. They're based on an organization's past, yet create its future. They describe the truth about an organization, yet they also change it.

But it can be done: many organizations have succeeded. What it takes is a readiness to live with these contradictions, to step outside the usual tramlines of thought and to listen to intuition.

Finding without searching

Some organizations begin life with an explicit big idea. The venture capital provider 3i, for instance, was founded in 1945 by the UK government, with the objective of encouraging the growth of small and medium-sized enterprises in Britain. From the beginning, the personalities of the people involved, and in particular that of John Kinross, made 3i – originally known as ICFC – into much more than just another hard-nosed merchant bank. 3i was infused by the idea that it existed not just to lend money but to kindle a whole economy, and that investment decisions are complex judgements about human nature. Gradually the people in 3i reflected on these principles and started to write them down. Out of a government policy goal grew a big idea about a very different kind of bank, an idea still palpable in 3i fifty years later.

3i started with a big idea. But for most organizations, the big idea emerges gradually over time. Howard Schultz of Starbucks says he didn't set out to create an idea or a brand – he set out to create a really good company, and everything else just developed. In fact, Starbucks was already 16 years old when Howard Schultz bought it. It had started life as a single outlet, in Seattle's open-air farmer's market, in 1971, and later began to emulate the espresso bars of Milan. As Howard Schultz expanded the business to over 2500 outlets, the Starbucks big idea became clear – a reinvention of the eighteenth-century coffee house as a social venue between home and work, with a wide choice of good coffee, comfortable sofas, newspapers, and a social conscience.

As management experts Chan Kim and Renee Mauborgne say, 'Starbucks changed coffee drinking from a commodity industry to an emotional experience.' Starbucks is the largest north American corporate donor to Care, the international relief agency. It recycles plastic cups, and gives you a discount if you bring your own mug. It gives all its employees, even part-timers, healthcare and share options, and it was one of the first American companies to treat same-sex partnerships the same way as heterosexual marriages.

In a sense, Starbucks stumbled on its big idea. For many years, it just did what it did, and then later encapsulated what it all meant.

The story of Virgin is an action adventure. It's all about going into things because it felt right at the time – a student magazine, then a record shop, then a music business, then an airline, and so on – and getting back out of them when things became too hairy. It's a kind of inspired opportunism. Virgin discovered its big idea just by doing all these things, and doing them in Sir Richard Branson's own particular spirit. 'More than any other element, fun is the secret of Virgin's success,' he says. 'I am aware that the idea of business being fun and creative goes right against the grain of convention, and it's certainly not how they teach it at some of those business schools, where business means hard grind and lots of "discounted cash flows" and "net present values".' Virgin has a big idea – about iconoclasm – because it's done everything in its own iconoclastic style. Idea is action.

Similarly, Ingvar Kamprad and his colleagues spent many years building IKEA before reflecting on the big idea behind the company, and writing it down as 'The IKEA Vision' and 'The IKEA Business Idea' in the mid 1970s. But Kamprad says, 'The basic thoughts of these ideas were already in my mind when I started my first business activities.' And the idea became clearer through a process of doing and reflecting. 'During the development of the company, I and my co-workers studied the home furnishing market, but it was not a kind of market research in the modern sense of the term. It has been and still is very much about learning while practising, to find different simple but smart solutions.'

Japanese retailer Muji started business at a time of high inflation, in the late 1970s, with the aim of selling clothes and housewares more cheaply. Out of that severely pragmatic beginning, a big idea unfolded: the idea that, to be economical to produce, the goods would be plain and simple; that plainness could be a virtue; that the products would be as natural as possible; that you could differentiate yourself by being a 'no-brand brand'; that people could use Muji products as a foundation on which to express their own individuality.

All these ideas emerged organically over time. But it's perfectly possible for an organization to set out deliberately to find one. And when it does, there's always a question about where to begin. Do you clarify the 'hard' things – strategy, structure and so on – before going in search of a big idea? Or must the big idea come first, and drive everything else?

The received wisdom is that the idea comes first.

Bob Garratt, in his exploration of the role of the board, *The Fish Rots From the Head*, is clear that what he calls 'policy' must come before strategy. 'Policy is about political will, or purpose,' he says. 'Strategy is about the broad deployment of resources to achieve this.' The board, in other words, must decide what the organization exists to do – the impact it wants to have on the world – before considering a strategy to achieve all this. And a big idea is very close to 'policy', because it's about the radical difference the organization wants to make.

That's the theory, but in practice it's messier than that. Most senior managers are more comfortable with facts and figures, with strategies and plans, than with big ideas and grand policies. It helps them to have some of these hard markers in the ground before they reflect on the big idea that the shape of those markers suggests. They may then, of course, want to move some of the markers. But somehow it feels easier to start with strategy, and to circle round to policy. To the question 'which comes first, strategy or idea?', there's a simple (but unhelpful) answer: strategy is the chicken, idea is the egg.

The same can be true of organizational structure. Should you clarify your big idea first, or design your organization's structure? The obvious theoretical answer is: idea first. But the people running an organization are only human. They need to know where they stand, if only temporarily. They need a structure to start from. And some structural arrangements are much more conducive to a successful search for a big idea than others. For example, a structure in which managers are rewarded purely on the success of their own business units creates a climate in

which people will fight for their corner, not look collectively
for a big idea.

Inside out

When organizations reflect on what they do – when they're
looking for their underlying big idea – where do they look?

The answer is both inside and outside their organization.
Inside, they look at what they've been doing, and what
seems to work best. They look at their own motives, and
at what excites their employees. But finding a big idea isn't
a process of navel-gazing. They equally look outside, talk
to customers, reflect on their industry and the wider world.
They think about what they love and what they hate about
their world. A big idea is, at least in part, a view of the
world. The important thing is that it's an *inwardly felt* view
of the outer world. It has to carry inner conviction.

Some big ideas start in the backgrounds of the people
leading the organization. London's Heathrow Express train
service, for instance, was created by an unusual – probably
unprecedented – mixture of airline and railway people. That
clash of cultures was the grain around which the Heathrow
Express pearl grew. The company brought many of the
service standards of an airline to the less glamorous world
of railways. But more important, it saw itself as providing
not just a short train journey, from Heathrow Airport to
Paddington Station in central London, but an integral stage
in a much longer air journey. It summed up the idea as
'1222 Delaware Avenue to 14 Acacia Road'. Out of the
mixed backgrounds of its founders, Heathrow Express built
a wider view of the world – a view that people have a right

to a complete and coherent journey. 'We don't consider the job done when we deliver a passenger to Paddington,' says chairman Alun Thomas. 'We organize taxi-sharing for instance, which has never been done in London before. It's about total responsibility even when you don't have total control. It's about coherence and completeness.'

Sometimes a big idea starts to take shape from the motives of the people involved. Britain's Channel 4 Television started with a bunch of disgruntled television producers in the early 1980s. Its current chief executive, Michael Jackson, was at that time a lobbyist on their behalf. 'It started with Michael Darlow and a number of other programme makers,' says Jackson. 'They were mavericks of one sort or another. We lobbied for Channel 4 because BBC and ITV were so corporatist – a duopoly. Television was very much a closed shop.' This desire for access to a closed shop was the starting point of Channel 4's big idea. What then emerged was a new television channel that, for the first time, commissioned programmes from independent production companies, rather than making them itself. And this distinctively different production structure helped shape a channel with a distinctively different view of the world. Starting from personal motives, Channel 4 found a big idea about 'difference' – about making programmes that were deliberately different from the mainstream, programmes that would reach minorities, programmes that might shock conventional taste.

This is a common pattern in the discovery of a big idea. Organizations start by looking at their own ambitions, interests and skills, and then find in the outside world a need, or a gap, or a challenge to map them on to. And importantly that outside-world need is a bigger one than anyone had spotted before. Heathrow Express identified the need not for a decent train service, but for complete and coherent journeys. Channel 4 identified the need not for yet another television channel but for 'difference' to be recognized and celebrated.

In a way, finding a big idea is therefore about widening the organization's arena, setting it on a much larger playing field. And when it starts to play in a bigger arena, an organization finds it faces new and unfamiliar competitors.

Many organizations with big ideas thrive on having a clearly defined enemy – and as big an enemy as possible. The team of people who created Orange defined themselves in relation to the existing mobile phone companies. 'We were an idealistic consortium, the rest were cowboys,' recalls Rob Furness. This determination to get it right, not to cut corners, was the source of Orange's big idea about freedom and optimism.

'It's more fun to be a pirate than to join the Navy,' said Steve Jobs of Apple. He saw Apple as a kind of outlaw in relation to the big computer companies of the 1970s, and compared the company to Ellis Island, a colony of refugees, of misfits. From this spirit of opposition grew Apple's big idea. It was not just against the big computer companies, but against giant corporations generally, and for the individual: 'We build a device that gives people the same power over information that large corporations and governments have had over people.'

The British daily newspaper the *Guardian* defines itself through a different kind of spirit of opposition. 'We're outsider rather than insider,' says its editor, Alan Rusbridger. 'We used to be defined by politics – we were seen as left-ish – but the truth is that the *Guardian* has always been an outsider. And what has always mattered most to us is trust. Readers have to trust the paper, have to feel it's free of influences that distort other papers. For example, we always own up to mistakes. We're not saying we can always present the truth, and we'll say when we've got it wrong.'

Of course, you don't have to be a pirate or an outsider to have a big idea. But big ideas are radical. They grow out of an inner drive to change an outer world. When an organization successfully finds its big idea, it does it by discovering in itself a view of the world, and of how that world could be better – more coherent, more diverse, freer, more individualistic, more truthful, richer, fairer, safer, more beautiful, more exciting.

And sometimes when an organization looks both outside and inside, it finds the same thing in both places. First Direct is built on a frustration shared by its founders and its customers – a frustration with traditional banking and a desire for something much better. The inside and the outside match. Indeed, First Direct looks for this feeling of frustration in both new employees and new customers. 'We're not a mass-market offering,' says Andrew Armishaw. 'We're looking for customers with a particular attitude – they feel frustrated with traditional banking and want to do something about it. And we empathize with that attitude.'

Though big ideas depend on a view of the market, they don't grow out of market research. They're built on a deep sense of new and unrecognized needs in the world, but organizations tend to understand those needs through intuition and common sense, rather than formal market research. Many chief executives are wary – if not actually dismissive – of market research.

'You can't research the future,' says Orange's Rob Furness. George Colony of Forrester Research agrees: 'The customer is a rear-view mirror, not a guide to the future.' People in focus groups know what they like, and like what they know: research tends to produce conservative, rather than radical, thinking.

Steve Jobs of Apple says it's the company's job to imagine the future, on behalf of customers. 'This is what customers pay us for – to sweat all these details so it's easy and pleasant for them to use our computers. We're supposed to be really good at this. That doesn't mean we don't listen to customers, but it's hard for them to tell you what they want when they've never seen anything remotely like it. Take desktop video editing. I never got one request from someone who wanted to edit movies on his computer. Yet now that people see it, they say "Oh my God, that's great!"'

Orange does carry out market research, but never allows it to dictate action: 'If I don't feel the same way as the research,' says Hans Snook, 'then maybe it's the research that's wrong.'

Richard Branson is famous for methodologically-unsound research. 'My staff are maddened to hear that I met a man on the airport bus who suggested that we offer on-board massages and please can they organize it. They tease me and call it "Richard's Straw Poll of One", but time and again the extra services which Virgin offers have been suggested to us by customers. I don't mind where the ideas come from as long as they make a difference.'

The real challenge, as Scott Bedbury of Starbucks says, is 'to peel back the layers of the customer – to get to his heart, his soul, to a place where he does not even think consciously. And to get there, you have to make decisions that you can't begin to justify financially – or even quantify – beforehand. You have to make these decisions from the gut, not based on focus groups or data. These are wild-card decisions – random thoughts or out-of-left-field observations.'

Back to the future

Big ideas are about the future. If they're not, they fail. IKEA saw, back in the 1970s, that the future lay in the democratization of design. Richard Branson felt, by intuition, that the new consumers of the 1970s, 1980s and 1990s would want to assert their individuality in the face of large, complacent companies. At a time when most people had never even seen a computer, Apple saw that they would become ubiquitous, and that it would be good if people loved them rather than fearing them.

What matters is not so much the accuracy of these intuitions as their passion. What matters is not whether the idea is 'right', but how deeply people believe it. Big ideas aren't about *predicting* the future. They have the power to *shape* the future.

That's what makes the journey towards a big idea so exciting. Though it's founded in the truth of the organization – its origins, its founding impulses, and the passions of its present-day people – it's all focused on a future that doesn't yet exist. It's an act, more than anything, of *imagination*.

'We've reached the limits of incrementalism,' say management experts Gary Hamel and C. K. Prahalad. 'Instead, the goal is to fundamentally reinvent existing competitive space (First Direct's telephone banking service in the United Kingdom) or invent entirely new competitive space (Netscape's Web browsers) in ways that amaze customers and dismay competitors . . . The goal is not to predict *the* future, but to imagine a future made possible by changes in technology, life style, work style, regulation, global geopolitics, and the like.'

How do organizations form passionate intuitions about the future? Some listen to today's equivalent of soothsayers – trend-watchers and research agencies. Some employ their own futurologists. Some use techniques like scenario planning, where groups of people get together to describe possible future events. Others simply live in the world, read books, see films, look at art, allow themselves to be influenced by people whose thinking is more personal than organizational.

And almost all think about the future by reflecting on their own past. Every big idea is also deeply rooted in its organization's past; that's what makes it belong distinctively to that organization. IKEA's big idea comes from its early years selling furniture in Sweden. Virgin's big idea sprang from Richard Branson's first record store, up a dark, narrow flight of stairs above a shoe shop in Notting Hill. Apple's big idea has always had a distinctly Californian feel to it. And Mandarin Oriental's big idea is Oriental: 'Having our heartland in the Orient has helped us to shape our culture,' says Edouard Ettedgui, chief executive officer. 'The idea of truly delighting your guest comes naturally to our people.'

To find a big idea, therefore, organizations simultaneously look into both the future and the past. In fact the two come together. As Max De Pree, chairman emeritus of American furniture maker Herman Miller, says: 'History can't be left to fend for itself. For when it comes to beliefs and values, we turn our future on the lathe of the past.'

Bang & Olufsen hit a financial crisis in 1993, after almost 70 years in business. Like many others at that time, it decided to downsize. The pain of downsizing stimulated a programme to discover, or rediscover, the big idea behind B&O. When you downsize a company, as Anders Knutsen found, people tend to ask 'can we survive?' What was it that had enabled B&O to survive for 70 years, and could it still work?

B&O's journey revealed that the company had been founded on the Bauhaus principles – a better product makes a better life – and that the company's big idea is about turning technology into concept. In Anders Knutsen's words, 'We reinvent hi-fi by giving it another expression.' That impulse gave B&O a new determination to be itself, and not to copy others, which brought the business back into profit.

Organizations can't help but be children of their time and place. Many organizations, in search of their big idea, have found it helpful to look back at the era in which they started life, or at the place they come from. Just as Virgin is an inescapably 1960s company, so Nokia is an inescapably Finnish business. 'Finns do not make a big noise about themselves,' says Mikael Frisk, vice-president of human resources. 'But there is an extraordinary determination to get things done quickly and without fuss. We do not just throw people in at the deep end, we also make sure the water is very cold – it encourages you to swim a bit faster.' It's this uniquely Finnish, alarmingly bracing quality that enables Nokia to introduce new products much faster – and in that way to shape, rather than just predict, the future.

Similarly, the *Guardian* newspaper has a big idea which is richly informed by its origins – which also happen to have a puritanical streak. The paper was founded in response to the Peterloo massacre, which occurred in Manchester in 1819 when supporters of parliamentary reform were attacked by soldiers, and eleven of them killed. 'We began as a Manchester paper, not a London paper, and therefore as an outsider,' says Alan Rusbridger, the editor. 'In 179 years, we've had only one owner: the *Guardian* has always been in the hands of slightly puritan figures who care about truth and trustworthiness.'

And Hewlett-Packard is currently turning its future on the lathe of its past. After a troubled period, Hewlett-Packard has rediscovered its original big idea – 'invention' – and is returning, emotionally, to its roots. The company started life in a garage in what's now known as Silicon Valley. Its advertising shows a garage, with glowing light inside, and proclaims: 'The original company of inventors started here. It is returning here. The original start-up will act like one again. From this day forward.' The style, unfortunately, is too bombastic. But the intention is sound: Hewlett-Packard is right to build its future on the foundation of its inventive past.

On the edge

Do big ideas all begin in the mind of a great charismatic leader? Does every big idea have its author, its hero, its founder? No: most big ideas are a collective product, and soon become a social property. And yet the collective effort seems to benefit from the presence of an individual who's prepared to shape, to cajole, to irritate – in a sense, to lead.

Many big ideas owe a lot to an individual. IKEA, Virgin and Apple are all good examples.

An important tool for decision-making comes into play here – one not often mentioned in business books – and that's *taste*. An individual's taste can drive a whole business, even change a whole industry. The big idea behind the American cookware retailer Williams Sonoma is essentially the taste of its founder, Chuck Williams. 'I just bought what I liked,' he admits. 'I never bought anything I didn't like. Fortunately there have been a lot of people out there who like what I like.'

Beyond taste, an individual's whole personality can shape a big idea. The low-cost airline Go owes a great deal to the personality of its first chief executive, Barbara Cassani.

But Barbara Cassani doesn't claim to be author of Go's big idea – it was a collective effort of doing what she and her colleagues felt to be right, and then reflecting on what they'd done. 'We had no battle plan,' she says. 'It was a very common-sense approach: to make the kind of airline we'd like to fly on ourselves. Many of us had worked for airlines and knew how hard they can make people's lives.' This collective impulse to make flying less hard, and in particular to create an airline without deference, turned the cool logic of British Airways into a warm, living, organic airline.

However energetic the corporate effort, it helps to have a guiding hand. For Hans Snook, the 200 or so people who created Orange were 'a bunch of people that wanted to do things differently, but had no context. I provided a sense of direction, I made it commercial.'

More and more new organizations are consortiums, joint ventures or virtual organizations of one sort or another. Here, the collective discovery of a big idea can be critical in giving the unformed entity a sense of itself. Yet it can still help to have one quietly guiding figure. For example, building a new city centre or a business park takes a complex virtual organization – developer, architect, letting agent, landscaper, surveyor, builder and so on. One such virtual organization – building a business park in London called Chiswick Park – found its identity by discovering a big idea about 'the right to enjoy work'. It was a collective discovery – yet it wouldn't have happened without the prodding of the lead developer, Sir Stuart Lipton. Finding a big idea is still a new, risky, dangerous thing to do in the highly traditional world of property. In workshop meetings, Stuart Lipton both admitted his fear and displayed his courage – 'OK, this is on the edge, but I like to be on the edge' – and this intervention was enough to persuade the whole virtual organization to find courage, take the risk, and unite behind this big idea.

Collective searches for a big idea fail if the chief executive abdicates responsibility. The boss doesn't have to be its immediate parent, but really should be present at the birth. One public agency in the UK spent six months searching for its big idea. Through interviews, workshops and email, almost everyone in the organization had a chance to contribute their opinion. The exercise unlocked a lot of energy in the organization, but the chief executive remained oddly detached from it. He expected the organization to present him with a big idea, which he would gratefully endorse. But it's not like that. A big idea needs the top person's conviction, not just their endorsement. A big idea must be social, but it must also be radical – and that, in the end, requires courage at the top. At some point in the search for a big idea, every chief executive has to say, 'OK, this is on the edge, but I like to be on the edge.' If an idea feels *comfortable*, it's probably not yet big enough.

Sixty minutes and sixty years

How long does it take to find a big idea? Because it's more a matter of instinct than research, it needn't, in theory, take long. Organizations sometimes find that an hour of productive reflection by their senior team can generate more than months of arduous interviews, workshops and symposia. And some organizations are set up with a clear and explicit purpose: for them the creation of the big idea, and the founding of the organization, happen together, and sometimes in a very short space of time.

Yet organizations and their worlds change over time. For some, the pursuit of a big idea takes decades: occasional prods by the outside world take them a step further forward. For others, a small but interesting idea gradually becomes relevant and urgent to the outside world: it becomes a big idea whose time has come.

To create the John Lewis Partnership, John Spedan Lewis gave away his family business to its employees. That single act revealed the big idea behind John Lewis – 'a better form of capitalism' – with labour employing capital instead of capital employing labour, and aiming for non-adversarial relationships with all its stakeholders. The National Trust was founded in 1895 to make open spaces accessible to city dwellers: its foundation revealed immediately its core idea

– protecting places of historic interest or natural beauty for the many to enjoy.

These two big ideas enjoyed a relatively short gestation. And yet both have grown – gained more dimensions – over time. Both organizations have survived and prospered and moved on, and in doing so have added to their original big idea. John Lewis has added new layers to 'a better form of capitalism', such as its pricing promise 'never knowingly undersold'. The National Trust is now better known for protecting country houses than open spaces. Both, interestingly, have become mainstream, part of the British establishment, almost institutions. But both are still, in their quiet and unassuming ways, radical. John Lewis is still the most successful model of a worker's co-operative, taking a stand against the fashion for demutualization. And the National Trust, in its current stand against hunting, is still prepared to challenge the countryside establishment. And, at the end of the twentieth century, both organizations were devoting significant effort to reformulating their big idea. John Lewis were rewriting their constitution in 'good, modern English', and the National Trust is working on 'a contemporary interpretation of the Trust's purpose'.

Shiseido, Japan's largest beauty products company, was similarly born with a big idea, and has added to it over the years. The company was set up in 1872 by Yushin Fuku-hara, former head pharmacist to the Japanese admiralty. The Japanese characters Shiseido mean 'praise the virtues of the earth, which nourishes new life and brings forth new values'. Big name, big idea. Yushin's third son, Shinzo, studied art in New York, and brought American thinking back to the company. Cosmetics replaced drugs as Shiseido's core business, and in 1921 Shinzo decided to make explicit the Shiseido big idea, in a set of five principles. The most striking is the fifth principle, 'we act in a spirit of thankfulness'.

By the late 1980s, Shiseido was Japan's leading cosmetics firm, and was starting to achieve success in the US market. It was still a family business, and the then president, Yoshiharu Fukuhara, worked with one of his vice-presidents, Akira Gemma, to define 'the Shiseido way'. This is a hierarchy of statements, incorporating the five principles, and starting with a corporate mission: 'We aim to identify new, richer sources of value and use them to create beauty in the lives and culture of those we serve.' These new words translate the original big idea into commitments to each of the company's five main stakeholder groups: they turn the big idea into a set of defined, and therefore measurable, relationships. They add a dimension to the big idea – but they don't replace or encapsulate it.

Everything changes

A journey to discover a big idea is a strange experience. Very rarely do organizations get straight there. They're much more likely to circle round, go two steps forward and one step back, discard something and then come back to it later. Often it's by looking inside themselves, and looking back at their origins, that they discover an idea about the future of the outside world. Their leader plays a paradoxical role – guiding, prodding, displaying courage, and yet making sure that the search is as collective as possible. And at some point, most organizations decide to write down the big idea, knowing that whatever gets written will be possibly inadequate, probably incomplete and certainly temporary.

Yet these journeys of discovery, or rediscovery, are also immensely exciting. Why? Because they change the organization. They are about finding the organization's soul, but they're not merely soul-searching – they're not an agonized process of self-analysis, ending more than likely in paralysis. They change things. The search changes the searcher.

By discovering what had been an implicit big idea, Starbucks found a formula that enabled it to grow spectacularly, from Seattle to the world. Virgin's big idea – though never quite explicit – enabled it to change its emphasis completely, from music business to airline in the 1980s, and now from airline to internet business, without losing an iota of its identity. Writing down IKEA's idea in the 1970s was the start of its global expansion. Finding the big idea behind Orange changed it from yet another mobile phone network to a new kind of communication company. The rediscovery of Tesco's big idea in the 1990s led to market leadership. Nokia's big idea took it from an ordinary Finnish papermaker to an extraordinary world communication company.

And often the journey changes the way the business is run for ever. Finding its big idea enabled Bang & Olufsen to make the switch from downsizing to growth, from loss to profit. But it also changed the business 'from a product-driven company to a vision-driven company', in Anders Knutsen's words. Put the big idea right at the centre of the organization – make it the touchstone for everything – and you have an amazingly effective new way to run the business.

The journey can be frustrating, even perilous. There is always a critical moment at which supreme courage is demanded – the courage to be on the edge, the courage not to be all things to all people. Yet the reward makes it worth it – the reward of becoming an organization that stands for something – a beacon in the marketplace.

CHAPTER SEVEN

crossing the shadows

Between the conception
And the creation
Falls the shadow.

You've found a big idea: one that aims to change the world. But there's a long way to go yet. The real task, as T. S. Eliot's lines suggest, isn't *conceiving* a big idea (discovering its content) but *creating* it (making it real). Making it real means, above all, engineering a shift in ownership.

What makes big ideas powerful is their multiple ownership: customers, employees, investors, suppliers feel that the big idea is *theirs*. Though a small group of insiders may *conceive* the big idea, it's that much wider community that *creates* it. That's how a big idea becomes a real force in the world.

Sony, Disney, Apple, IKEA, Virgin: all of them have enlisted millions of people to *create* their big idea. All have a big idea that's a piece of social property, part of the social fabric.

But between the conception and the creation falls the shadow. Ideas are fragile, and all sorts of things get in the way, and darken the path.

There's the shadow of boredom: if an exciting idea is *written down* in dull, dead words, or in management jargon, people react with indifference or boredom. And if a great idea becomes too complicated, people can't grasp or remember it.

And the shadow of dissonance: if the idea is *expressed* in a style or tone that seems to contradict it, people react with confusion.

And the shadow of oblivion: if the idea isn't *communicated* in an engaging enough way to the outside world, people simply don't know about it.

And the shadow of resistance: if the organization *reinforces* its big idea in a way that's too evangelistic, too monotonous, too strident, people bridle and put up barriers. Insiders may feel that it's only a year since they heard the organization's previous vision; outsiders may feel overwhelmed by ideas, words, slogans, catch-phrases from the organizations that fill their lives.

And, finally, the shadow of cynicism: if the organization says one thing but acts differently, people become cynical.

This may sound overwhelming. It isn't. All you have to do is step across the shadows. Many organizations have succeeded. How have they managed it? What does it take to make a radical idea into a piece of social property?

First, the organization finds a way of expressing the idea that makes sense to people – that uses words and phrases and images that are potent, but also that belong to the everyday world. It aims for an expression that's simple, but not one-dimensional. Its style reinforces its message. It finds an ordinary eloquence.

Second, it uses the idea to inspire people. With a great deal of energy, it gets the idea out into the world. But that doesn't mean lecturing people. It's much more to do with *showing* the idea than telling it. It finds completely new ways of engaging people. Its leaders visibly live the idea.

Gradually, as more and more people 'get it' – and apply it to their own lives – it becomes a social property. And those people feel more and more like active *members* of the organization.

Ordinary eloquence

The first, and most pervasive, shadow is boredom. Too many organizations have found an idea, but *written it down* in such a tedious way that it's never become big. No one has ever become excited by it.

Perhaps surprisingly, the best way to avoid boredom is not to try too hard. It's not a matter of striving for the extraordinary. The biggest big ideas live in the everyday world of ordinary words. They may seem naïve, almost vulnerable. They may never get written down. But they have an ordinary eloquence. The one thing they're not is boring.

Tesco's simple core thought, for instance, is 'we like our customers'. Nothing could be less complicated or less pretentious. It's emphatically not a slogan: imagine how feeble an advertisement would sound that ended with that strapline. It doesn't even appear on Tesco's official purpose statement: it's a phrase that comes across much better when dropped into conversation. And yet from it grows the whole world of Tesco. Because it's so simple and universal, it's a thought that works just as well in Thailand as in Tottenham.

It's so straightforward, and yet so full of implications, that it can never be boring. The same is true of the business park whose big idea is 'the right to enjoy work'. Or of Sony and 'miniature perfection'. Or of Disney's 'we sell fun'. Or of Orange and its optimism.

More often than not, however, organizations attempt to be extraordinary by using extraordinary words – the management hyperbole of 'global', 'excellence', 'passion' and so on, words rarely used in everyday conversation. But the effect, maddeningly, is to be instantly forgettable – to sound the same as everyone else, to say nothing uplifting, to be banal.

The temptation, too, is to use management mantras about 'risk-taking', 'teamwork', 'creating value', 'innovation', 'leadership', 'integrity' and 'partnership'. Again, the result is dead on the page – these phrases have little resonance in ordinary life. This, as the French say, is *langue du bois*. It's as dead, and as indigestible, as dead wood.

And this dead language, although it's everywhere at the moment, is starting to feel very old-fashioned. 'In just a few more years,' say the writers of *The Cluetrain Manifesto*, which analyses the cultural implications of the internet economy, 'the current homogenized "voice" of business – the sound of mission statements and brochures – will seem as contrived and artificial as the language of the eighteenth-century French court.'

Achieving the right level of ordinariness, without merely being mundane, may seem hard to do. The risks are real: you may come across as simple-minded, or out of touch with commercial realities. You may even be laughed at. But it can be done. It's perfectly possible to express a big idea in ordinary words. The venture capital provider 3i has an exemplary booklet setting out its big idea. It starts in an engaging way:

Every company has its own way of doing things. When you work somewhere you know intuitively, after a while, what 'feels right' or 'feels wrong'. It's part of the ethos of the company.

The same is true of our company. This booklet expresses the special and different way we do things.

This, in other words, is a big idea that's *social* and *tangible* – not a piece of management wishful thinking. Later in the booklet, the *radical* side of the big idea becomes apparent. This is a venture capital firm that really believes in integrity:

A useful guide to whether you've got it right is to ask yourself the following question: Would I be happy to explain my reasons to every party involved?

And the booklet ends quite unexpectedly, in a different diction altogether – with a specially written poem by Christopher Logue:

> *Come to the edge.*
> We might fall.
> *Come to the edge.*
> It's too high!
> *COME TO THE EDGE!*
> *And they came,*
> *and he pushed,*
> > *and they flew.*

This may not be the greatest poetry, but what it does is to take 3i's statement of its big idea into another dimension. It takes it out of the management car-park, into people's lives. It sends them back into childhood. It makes its readers remember what it's like to take risks. Through it, readers re-live the experience of danger: they remember how things often turn out to be much less frightening than you expect, and much more exhilarating. All of which is a completely different thing from merely scanning the tired old words 'risk-taking', processing them along the usual neural channels, and assenting superficially and automatically to the virtues of taking risks. With Logue's poem, 3i stops making a statement and starts imagining a world – which is what anyone trying to express a big idea has to do. There's a knack to achieving plain and simple eloquence. It's the knack of throwing things away.

Every organization, when thinking about its big idea, digs up a huge range of thoughts, quotations, anecdotes, statistics, points of view. Many, driven by a spirit of completeness, want to generate a sort of corporate catechism, with statements of vision, purpose, mission, ambition and values. But no one can take all that in. Instead, be simple. Discard. Throw away everything but the essentials. Then throw away some of the essentials too.

Disney's core thought is, simply, 'fun'. Nike's core thought is 'winning'. From these simple core thoughts, they've imagined whole worlds.

This is the hardest part of the whole big idea business: narrowing things down, finding that simple truth. Most managers are taught to assimilate – to gather every available fact and take each one into account. And if an organization brings in management consultants to advise them, it usually finds that those consultants are *obsessed* with assimilation – the consultant's nightmare is to miss out something significant. But every organization with a big idea has, at some stage, operated in the opposite way – sometimes deliberately, but usually unconsciously. It has taken an instinctive view of what matters, and has let everything else go. It has been happy to throw things away. It may be clever to collect, but the real genius is to discard.

Often the spirit of assimilation has a worthwhile aim: to find an idea that can unite all the organization's stakeholders. The thinking is that if you assimilate everyone's views, and take everyone's interests into account, you'll end up with an idea that will galvanize everyone. Everyone will recognize in it something they contributed.

But it doesn't work that way: upsetting no one means exciting no one. Assimilation produces the bland statements of vision and mission that we're all so used to: assimilation never produces big ideas. Big ideas work the other way.

By standing for everything – and so upsetting no one – an organization wins, at best, acceptance or approval from large numbers of people. More likely, it simply doesn't get noticed. But by standing for something – and that usually means antagonizing one group or another – the organization can gain a much higher profile, and then a much deeper level of commitment from the people that matter most: the customers and employees it really wants.

Expressing a big idea, then, doesn't mean covering all the bases, incorporating everyone's contribution, lumping things together. It means ruthlessly discarding, until you arrive at something simple.

Imagine a world

The second shadow – dissonance – is in some ways the strangest. An organization may express its idea with ordinary eloquence, and it may have achieved an admirable level of simplicity. But somehow the way it puts the idea across conflicts with what it's trying to say. The *what* and the *how* fight each other.

A good example is British Airways, whose idea, it says, is about world travel. It wants to be a complete travel provider for the whole world. It wants to be more than British and more than airways. Yet its name is still 'British Airways'. Its logo is still red, white and blue. And it's even dropping its ethnic tailplane designs in favour of a stylized Union Jack flag. This is dissonance. It's now very hard to tell what British Airways is about. At the moment, it doesn't have a big idea.

Another example is Benetton. Its idea seems to be about humanity. That's why its advertising shows Aids patients and death-row prisoners: we're all human underneath, it suggests. Yet its products and stores don't say anything in particular about humanity, beyond the notion of 'the united colors of Benetton'. There's a huge idea there, but there's dissonance in the way the idea is brought to life.

To prevent dissonance, the solution is not to write a statement of the big idea, but to imagine the whole world of which it's the core. This means thinking deliberately about all the ways the organization comes across – its tone of voice, its communication style, what it looks like, its products, its services, its places, and how its people behave

– and imagining how they all ought to be, if they're going to express the big idea consistently. And it's not just consistency that's needed: it's a deeper unity of feeling.

Needless to stay, getting the style right is no substitute for the big idea itself. An organization can be totally consistent, totally coherent, and yet have no big idea. Uniformity, interestingly, isn't the same thing as unity. Swissair, for instance, is extraordinarily coherent, but it doesn't have a big idea. It's great to be coherent, uniform, tidy, but that's not the same thing as being unified and excited.

Getting engaged

You may have achieved ordinary eloquence. You may have plans to prevent dissonance. But the real challenge now is to get all this out into the world. Otherwise, the third shadow, oblivion, inevitably falls: people just won't notice your big idea.

The way to do this is, simply, to engage with people. To get to them, to get under their skins, to provoke a reaction. And to do that through as many different communication channels as possible. This doesn't necessarily mean spending millions on blanket coverage that will reach consumers everywhere. It does mean devoting energy to reaching the people who matter most.

People relate much more easily to other people than to ideas. It's therefore no surprise that many of the biggest big ideas around at the moment are closely linked to particular individuals. Most notably, Virgin's big idea is personified by Richard Branson. The media are constantly searching for other individuals they can use to put flesh on an organization – Jeff Bezos for Amazon, Howard Schultz for Starbucks, and so on.

These human icons of a big idea are becoming much more common. 'There's something new and daring about the CEOs who are transforming today's industries,' reports the *Harvard Business Review*. 'Just compare them with the executives who ran large companies in the 1950s through the 1980s. Those executives shunned the press and had their comments carefully crafted by corporate PR departments. But today's CEOs – superstars such as Bill Gates, Andy Grove, Steve Jobs, Jeff Bezos and Jack Welch – hire their own publicists, write books, grant spontaneous interviews and actively promote their personal philosophies.' They do all of this because they know that it's the best way to make their organization's big idea into something social. People engage with GE because they engage with Jack Welch. They see Amazon as special because they watch the actions and the pronouncements of Jeff Bezos.

And part of the great power of these people is that they engage both employees and customers at the same time and in the same way. Indeed, what they say and do gains a lot of its credibility for insiders simply because it's so visible to outsiders.

But crossing the shadow of oblivion means more than finding someone to personify the big idea. Big ideas also need big communication. They need to be proclaimed.

Advertising is the obvious way to do that. Nike in many ways *is* its advertising, and its style is so unmistakable that its adverts don't need the word 'Nike'. Every ad proclaims (without preaching) the idea of winning. It challenges. It engages.

This kind of advertising reaches insiders as well as out-

siders, employees as well as customers. It gives them a new
self-image. Britain's biggest roadside rescue organization,
the AA, has a big idea: it's 'the fourth emergency service'.
And it used advertising to make this idea social – to make
it real for insiders as well as outsiders. 'AA staff now see
themselves as more than just "very nice people",' reports
management expert Kevin Thomson. They see themselves
as 'a part of something deeper, more passionate, more
inspired. They see themselves as another vital emergency
service.'

But big communication doesn't have to have a big
budget. Other organizations seize every opportunity to pro-
claim their idea. Small touches add up to big impact.

When you buy a Bang & Olufsen hi-fi, for instance, you
get more than the usual instruction manual. There's a letter
from Anders Knutsen headed 'Now that we are going to live
together . . .' in which he talks about his own excitement at
getting his first B&O product, and says 'so I think I have
an idea of how you feel right now'. This is engagement, in
its most direct form. And there's a booklet that shows the
B&O big idea, starting: 'This is the brief story of a small
business that made its claim to fame by insisting on producing quality in every aspect of their manufacture.' In effect,
the booklet says 'this is a company that cares deeply about
more than just the hardware'. It's small budget, but big
communication.

Similarly, Heathrow Express starts communicating with
customers the moment they get off their plane. Arrows on
the airport floor point them towards the train station. This
is advertising that doesn't *talk about* the Heathrow Express
big idea – seamless travel – but instead helps to *deliver* it. It
doesn't just preach to people: it engages them.

But the biggest communication often comes from things that can't themselves speak – the organization's products and services.

The iMac is an icon of Apple's big idea. The new Beetle is in many ways a similar icon for Volkswagen. The Walkman has symbolized Sony for two decades. By using, driving, listening to one of these icon products, you inevitably engage with the big ideas behind them.

Media companies with a big idea can make particularly powerful use of their product. Every day, the *Guardian* shows the world (and reminds employees) what the *Guardian* stands for. This is a business that scarcely needs a statement of its idea (or vision or mission or whatever): it publishes something every day that embodies it. 'You don't have to instil it in people,' says editor Alan Rusbridger. 'People are already familiar with the *Guardian* when they come to work here.' Similarly, organizations that publish things – whether books like Penguin or television programmes like Channel 4 – can pick particular products from their output and hold them up as icons of what they stand for.

All of these routes – prominent personalities, powerful advertising, iconic products – start to bring people inside. They don't just talk, they engage. It's a two-way thing. And that's how a big idea can start to become a social property.

Indirect line

All of this communication puts an organization's big idea out into the world. But now the fourth shadow starts to fall: resistance.

People instinctively resist new ideas if they feel that you're preaching at them, or boasting to them. And in all probability, your employees are still reeling from your previous vision statement, or change programme, or benchmarking exercise, or reorganization, or divestment, or acquisition. Meanwhile, your customers are bombarded every day by hype and spin, by over-inflated messages and by portentous slogans.

The only way to cross the fourth shadow is obliquely. Communicate indirectly. Let people make up their own minds: that's what enables people to make the idea *theirs*. And enlist the help of time. A big idea is not a quick fix: it's a long-term investment. Most organizations with a big idea let it grow gradually over time. The world may be changing faster than ever – or so we are incessantly told – but a big idea is a five-year, or even a fifty-year, project.

Shell's approach, for instance, is too heavy-handed. Shell wants to be seen as a responsible citizen, committed to sustainable development, the environment and human rights. But its advertising doesn't dramatize that idea: it baldly states it. And its annual Shell Report – which could be an engrossing survey of the whole idea of sustainability – is instead a barrage of examples of what Shell has got right (and, to be fair, what it has got wrong). The overriding impression created by this communication is of an organization that's more interested in itself than it is in sustainability.

Indirect communication works better. Many organizations produce publications that talk not about themselves but about the outside world – but, in doing that, imply a great deal about their own big idea. British supermarket chain Waitrose publishes a monthly glossy magazine about food, illustrated with the kind of photography you'd find in a fashion magazine. It rarely mentions Waitrose products. Instead it imagines a whole world of foods and flavours, from the organic farm to the restaurant table. It implies that Waitrose is part of that world, and makes its customers members of that club. Much more famously, the management consultants McKinsey produce a management journal, the *McKinsey Quarterly*, which conveys new thinking – illustrated with scientific-looking diagrams – to its exclusive club of subscribers. The *McKinsey Quarterly* is McKinsey in microcosm. And the in-flight magazine on Go isn't a magazine at all: it's a short and helpful guide to the city you're about to visit. Importantly, the guide covers, quite unselfconsciously, the more expensive attractions as well as the cheapest. Implicitly it says: 'Go isn't for cheapskates, it's for people who know what they want.'

Many organizations now organize conferences – often on subjects only loosely related to their core business. The insurance company Winterthur, for example, runs a conference every other year: most recently, a two-day event in Interlaken surveyed world issues 'on the threshold of the 21st century', with international statespeople like Nobel Peace Prize winner Shimon Perez, and UN Commissioner for Human Rights Mary Robinson. The value of these conferences – apart from the media coverage they attract – is the way they demonstrate the organization's interest in something beyond its narrow commercial goals.

Indirect communication takes time. But then a big idea is a long-term investment.

It's true that, by communicating engagingly – and, more importantly, by doing what they claimed to do – some organizations have made their big idea into a social property very rapidly. Orange is one example, Amazon another. In the markets where they operate, both have become part of the daily social vocabulary.

But most big ideas have grown over decades: think of Sony, or McKinsey, or John Lewis. They've steadfastly lived out their big idea, rather than bombarding people with it. They haven't taken short cuts.

One tempting short cut is the launch event – a big announcement to employees. But that makes the big idea look like yet another initiative. It's not an initiative, it's the soul of the organization. People reveal their souls slowly over time: they don't get everyone together and show them a video.

Another short cut is the slogan. In just a few words, it's tempting to suppose, you could feed a big idea in a bite-sized chunk to tired employees and sated customers. Indeed, almost every organization these days has a strapline. Many are ludicrous, like the English county 'where partnership works'. Most are a bit more inventive, but they won't work as a short-cut to making a big idea into a social property.

It's true that a great deal of Orange's big idea is captured in its original advertising line 'the future's bright, the future's Orange'. But slogans usually have a much shorter lifespan than a big idea, and can at best express only one aspect of that idea. Apple's 'think different' says a lot about Apple – particularly through its laid-back attitude to grammatical correctness – but it can't say everything.

And the trend at the moment in slogans is to downsize to just two or three words, like 'Volvo for life' or 'United Airlines rising', in the belief that attention spans are getting ever shorter. This rigorous verbal economy may help to get across an advertising message in an increasingly verbose world, but it makes it still harder for a slogan to be an adequate expression of a big idea. 'Volvo for life' is bland, or would be if it didn't gain stature from Volvo's commitment over the decades to safety. 'United Airlines rising' (or, as it's sometimes written, 'United is rising') is wishful thinking at best, and rather sinister at worst. You can't take a short cut to a big idea.

Live it

One risk from short cuts is that they can take you into the fifth and darkest shadow: cynicism. Organizations have never been under greater scrutiny, by both outsiders and insiders. If an organization fails to live up to its big idea, people will notice. They will suspect that the organization doesn't really believe in its big idea. And they certainly won't want to make that idea their own.

The only way to counter cynicism is with integrity. The organization must live the big idea.

That starts with its leaders. In most organizations, what the leaders do – their decisions, their gestures, their emotions – sends a signal about what the organization should do. Employees don't merely interpret, they also copy what their top people do. 'The company watches senior management,' says Disney's Michael Eisner. Employees 'look to us as role models. So each one of us should work very, very hard at living up to that.' Michael Eisner mentions one particular example. 'In the middle of a meeting on financial performance, I may say, ''My wife and I were in Disneyland Paris two weeks ago. Alice's Maze is just not exciting enough. What can we do?'' They'll look at me like ''How did Alice's Maze get into this meeting? We were talking about return on equity.'' But what I am showing is that any and all questions are fair game.' What matters most to Disney, in the end, is just how exciting Alice's Maze is. Disney's big idea is about fun. Michael Eisner's behaviour is designed to get everyone in Disney to put fun first.

But leaders don't have to be big people to inspire their colleagues. Most organizations with a big idea don't have a famous chief executive. But they all – without exception – have a chief executive who believes in the big idea, and who lives it day by day.

Smaller organizations can get yet more personal. Everyone who joins Go goes to see Barbara Cassani, its chief executive, and she gives them a special Go watch. She sends everyone a signed birthday card – a big job in its own right. 'We have great parties', she says, 'and we treat subcontractors just like staff.' In all of these ways, Barbara Cassani acts as a personification of the Go big idea, which is about caring for everyone equally. 'It's the hug principle,' she says. And it all has a commercial purpose. 'All our people really care – that's why we recruited them – and that's my only secret weapon.'

None of these people operate by rote. They live out the big idea because they believe in it. Insincerity is easy to detect, and once detected it's fatal. As Michael Eisner says, 'Who we are as people matters as much as what we do.' Or as the Australian Aborigines put it, 'You must become the change you want to see in the world.'

Leaders send signals. But so, just as powerfully, do all the ordinary things that happen day by day in an organization – the nitty-gritty.

In organizations with a big idea, the nitty-gritty lives out that idea – in both the letter and the spirit – and provides a daily counter to cynicism.

The way that Southwest Airlines recruits people is a good example. Candidate pilots are vetted – so the story goes – not just by the interviewing panel, but also by the receptionist who greets them when they arrive for their interview. If candidates are warm and human when off-guard – if they behave with natural friendliness to the receptionist – then they get through to the next stage of the selection process. If they're self-important or brusque, they won't get a job. Genuine friendliness to everyone is central to Southwest's big idea – and it's just as important a qualification for senior pilots as it is for junior flight attendants.

Disney runs a regular programme called Disney Dimensions. 'It's like a synergy boot camp,' says Michael Eisner. Senior employees, twenty-five at a time, go through eight long gruelling days of meetings and activities, travelling between headquarters in California, Disneyland, ABC in New York and Disney World in Florida. They meet colleagues, see presentations, greet guests, clean bathrooms, cut hedges. But by the time they've finished, synergy – collaborating with colleagues – comes naturally. For those who attend, the event is of huge practical benefit. But it also has a force for those who don't attend. It says that Disney is all about creating multi-dimensional fun – delivering any given creative idea through films, theme parks, television shows, websites, merchandizing, and anything else you can think of.

In some organizations, these practices are elevated to the stature of rules. At McKinsey, the 'obligation to dissent' is an unwritten rule. Employees are expected, when they disagree about something, to say so. The practice is symbolic of the critical intelligence that the firm offers its clients.

At Mandarin Oriental hotels, the big idea is encapsulated in a manual called *Legendary quality experiences*, which gives 150 basic 'moments of delight', covering each step in a guest's experience of a hotel. The important point about this book is that it records how staff actually behave: it's not a manual that staff are expected to follow mechanically. For example, one rule states that, in restaurants or bars, 'Guests will never have to initiate a request for anything.' Edouard Ettedgui, chief executive officer, says, 'We can say that in the LQE because that's what our people are doing anyway.'

These kinds of practices aren't occasional events, but part of the internal climate of the organization. The same is true of the way that the British retailer John Lewis is run. John Lewis is an employee-owned co-operative, whose big idea is about a non-adversarial way of doing business. Employees have many democratic rights, including deciding on store opening hours. Of necessity, there are all sorts of committees and bureaucratic procedures to run the business, but John Lewis makes a virtue of these necessities, and uses them to demonstrate the big idea. 'Management's objective', says chairman Sir Stuart Hampson, 'is constantly to make people feel like owners.' And this is almost subliminally visible to customers too: the doors that lead off the sales floor to the stock rooms are marked not 'staff only' but 'partners only'. Each time customers glimpse one of these signs, they register that this is a special kind of business, and that the sales assistants they talk to have a special kind of commitment to it.

What matters about these practices is their indirect force. 'It doesn't work to go out and make big ethical statements,' says Thomas Wellauer of Credit Suisse. 'It's much better to be indirect. And it's the small signals you send – for example, the fact that there's no small print in your insurance documents – that carry the greatest credibility.'

The people at Heathrow Express talk about one example of a small signal. 'We have one regular customer who flies to London from Belfast,' says Alun Thomas, Heathrow Express's chairman, 'and he's disabled. Normally it's a big problem for him to get through the barriers at the station in his wheelchair, because they're locked for security reasons. So we've given him a key.' A small gesture, but a big symbol – not only of the Heathrow Express idea of seamless travel, but also of the way that organizations with a big idea are destroying the distinction – unlocking the barrier – between insiders and outsiders.

Through all these ways – many of them very small – an organization lives, and is seen to live, its big idea, and can therefore prevent, or counter, cynicism.

The other side of the shadow

Once an organization has crossed the shadow, exciting things start to happen.

The organization has moved from 'conception' to 'creation'. And it's not the chief executive who's doing the creating – it's employees, customers, investors, advisers, even the media. The idea is now owned by people outside as well as inside the organization: emotionally, that distinction has started to become irrelevant. The big idea has become folklore.

And a network effect comes into play. As with folklore,

people pass it on – in their own terms, their own words, and with their own emotional commitment.

Inside the organization, the big idea gets 'passed down'. Employees become enthusiasts. Outside, 'word-of-mouth' spreads it like wildfire. Customers become advocates. Both carry infinitely more credibility than any official pronouncements. And both are now being speeded up by electronic chat.

All this talk makes the organization into a community, a club, a society. People feel they belong. This isn't the fake membership created by loyalty schemes or air mile programmes. In fact, it's not merely loyalty that's created but a much deeper belief.

At 3i, the big idea booklet, with the Christopher Logue poem as its climax, is important. 'But', says chief executive Brian Larcombe, 'it's not something that people actually read very often. The real thing happens in the pub on a Friday night. A senior person says, "I'm working on x, here are some of the issues, what should we do?", and that's how people really get to understand about 3i . . . It's all passed down from generation to generation.'

John Lewis has crossed the shadow too. 'The philosophy', says Sir Stuart Hampson, its chairman, 'is deeply ingrained. It's something people assimilate.'

At the *Guardian*, journalists spread the big idea by talking – mostly about what was or wasn't in yesterday's paper. 'We have a high stability of staff – there's very little churn,' says Alan Rusbridger. 'This means that young people can learn a lot from old-timers by osmosis.'

Passing down, assimilation, osmosis: that's how a big idea really takes off. Usually, the chat is about current practical things – How do we handle this client? What should

I do about that customer? Were we right to run that story? But sometimes it's informed by stories – examples of recent instances, or stories about the early days of the company.

'At some companies,' says leadership expert Max De Pree, 'people come to understand that corporate tribalism lies at the heart of why so many people from such a variety of cultures make over the years such unusual contributions to corporate life.' De Pree, who used to run furniture maker Herman Miller, adds: 'These people realize the value of tribal storytellers, the custodians of the history and values and culture of any group.' Nike has its own 'corporate storytellers': senior people who go round telling employees the story of the company's past. This sounds worryingly like the Ancient Mariner, buttonholing defenceless wedding-guests with endless corporate sagas. And too much talk about the past can turn what was once a lively big idea into a deadly ideology – a world in which there's only one right way to do things. But stories can work – when they illustrate the big idea and help people better understand how to apply it to today's pressing problem.

Passing down – osmosis – happens with outsiders, such as suppliers, too. Part of the secret behind Southcorp's most famous wine, Grange, is the dialogue between Southcorp and its growers. 'We get Grange growers together, and build up a spirit,' says Southcorp's Bruce Kemp. 'It's aspirational – it feels like a club.'

The telephone bank First Direct was launched by a set of deliberately odd poster advertisements, showing images like a row of milk bottles that seemed to have nothing to do with banking. To the vast majority of people, these posters were puzzling at best, irritating at worst. But to the bank's first target customers – early adopters frustrated by traditional banking – they stood for something new and very different. They almost challenged these people to sign up. And early adopters, if they like what they find, quickly become efficient advocates. First Direct's early adopters were amazed by the level of service the bank could provide, and told their friends about it. The word-of-mouth spread began. The First Direct idea became a social property. And throughout its life, First Direct has gained, mainly by word-of-mouth, around 10,000 new customers a month.

The internet makes it easier than ever for these conversations to happen. Email is the most effective medium for word-of-mouth ever: messages can multiply faster, and reach further round the world, than is possible through chats in bars or on the phone. But there are even more effective electronic methods than email.

Inside organizations, for example, people are now using internal websites to find out about their organization's big idea, and in particular to work out how best to apply it to their particular problem. They then add their solution on to the website, which gives the next visitor a slightly richer picture of the big idea and what it means. The big idea lives in electronic space, belonging to no one and everyone.

Outside organizations, customers can talk, compare notes, suggest improvements to products and services, even design their own products and services. In many cases, these customer-contributors are simply enhancing the organization's product or service. But in more and more cases, they are also adding to its big idea. *Guardian* editor Alan Rusbridger sees readers in the near future contributing their own content to his on-line edition. Once that happens – unless contributions are ruthlessly censored – the

Guardian's big idea will become a much more public property than it's ever been before.

The inside-outside distinction is further disappearing as everyone gains access to the same websites. Customers, employees, suppliers – and whoever else – are coming together in virtual communities.

This kind of organization isn't a traditional corporation at all, but a host. It's perfectly possible to be a neutral, self-effacing host, letting the chat happen around you. But the best ones will be like society hostesses, sparking off the liveliest conversations by injecting a point of view of their own. The best ones, in other words, will have a big idea, and then – through every means, electronic and otherwise – let it loose, invite agreement, argument and emendation. By becoming a social property, it will live.

That's the nirvana that the best organizations are now aiming for. A world in which all their people buy into their big idea – not in a mindless, uncritical way but in a highly active way that enhances, rather than diminishes, their individuality. Making a big idea social is about finding every way not of demanding loyalty but of inspiring action.

CHAPTER EIGHT

the seven ages of a big idea

Solomon Grundy
Born on a Monday
Christened on Tuesday
Married on Wednesday
Ill on Thursday
Worse on Friday
Dead on Saturday
Buried on Sunday
And that was the end of
Solomon Grundy

Most organizations live a life that's all too brief. On some calculations, the average lifespan of a multinational organization is forty to fifty years. Can an organization with a big idea do better, and live longer? And if so, how?

There's a secret to staying alive: to treat the big idea not as the answer but the *question*. Organizations with a big idea use it to keep asking questions – about what it means, about how best to live it, about what they could improve on, about what they should stop doing, about what they need to rethink from scratch. A big idea is a continuous challenge – a challenge for life.

These simple questions change over time. As an organization grows, evolves, changes, merges, splits up, so different threats emerge. The best way to live the big idea changes.

It's hard to generalize, but there are probably seven phases in the life of an organization: the seven ages of a big idea.

1. The hyperactive child

For a fledgling organization, the first ten years flash past. There's a lot going on, in a lot of different directions. Most days present tantalizing new opportunities, or disturbing new threats. It's all action: indeed, it's almost hyperactive. The urgent constantly displaces the important. Some tasks start to become routine. But at the same time, new people are keen and impatient: many want to change things, to do them their way, but find that the organization already has its own rules and methods.

'There's a constant challenge to make it feel like more than a job,' says Alun Thomas of Heathrow Express. 'It's harder to maintain passion internally, now that the service is no longer a baby but a gawky adolescent – particularly as there are now some norms that people feel they can't challenge or change.'

Success brings the risk of dilution. As the organization grows, more and more people become involved, and they each bring their own interpretation of the idea. Gradually, the original thought becomes weakened, diluted.

'It's easy to go off track, to forget where you came from,' agrees Hans Snook of Orange. 'The danger is new people coming in who don't really understand Orange, and who want to change bits of Orange.' So how does Orange deal with the problem? 'We manage it by worrying at it – always knowing that it's not quite there.' Managing by worrying, by restlessness, by asking questions.

And the messy day-to-day problems of running an organization can distract people's attention from the big idea. Maybe one or two of the founders move on. Good intentions get forgotten. A lack of confidence may mean that the organization fails to exploit the big idea, and sticks with what's safer and more familiar. Organizational entropy sets in.

Many chief executives don't invest the time to keep the idea alive and fresh. Other issues get more priority. Other issues, significantly, have someone on the board to look after them. Things therefore happen under the headings of IT or human resources or marketing: but the big idea disappears into the wallpaper.

The question in these early years is how to prevent this entropy, this dilution, this watering-down.

The main answer for many organizations in these early years is new people: bringing in employees who will stiffen, rather than dilute, the mix.

Heathrow Express takes emotions very seriously. To live its idea of seamless travel, it needs people who'll make the most ruffled passenger feel calm, feel that everything's being taken care of. 'We use an application form', says Alun Thomas, 'that requires people to talk about times they got angry and how they handled it. And applicants go through an assessment centre, with professional actors role-playing distressed customers. One day, one of our actors wasn't being angry enough. When we challenged him, he said, "I don't do anger, I only do seething from within".'

Virgin Atlantic, in its early days, recruited equally carefully. Salaries weren't great, but the right kinds of people were keen to join. And Virgin picked out the best by looking for 'informal but caring' people – young, vibrant, interested and courteous.

Pret a Manger uses employees to select employees – a process that requires its people to think hard about what kinds of new people are right for the organization. Promising candidates are paid to do a day's work experience in an outlet near where they live. They go home at 4 pm, and the rest of the staff vote for or against them on napkins. Only one in five get a job. So Pret a Manger people get to choose new Pret a Manger people. The result, says chairman Julian Metcalfe, is that 'I've got a group of people around me who understand that the spirit of the organization is what matters.'

And Orange goes out of its way to expose new employees to the Orange idea. 'Every time we talk about what Orange is doing, we pull in new people, we get them involved – it's a constant thought process. I often talk about what's Orange and what isn't. We look at recent work – maybe an advertising campaign in a country we've just gone into. I pick out the wrong notes. It's like a piece of music: you've never heard it before, but you know it's a wrong note.'

The first age is an age of concentration: keeping the mixture rich by bringing in the right new people, and teaching them to hear the wrong notes.

2. The awkward age

Emerging from the early years, many organizations hit an awkward age. They've avoided dilution: indeed, they've successfully been very single-minded. But the danger is that, as a result, they've become one-dimensional.

The question in this second age is: with our big idea,

what else can we do? The answer is to unpack the big idea, to discover what more it can mean, and to translate all that into new services or new products.

As it hit its tenth birthday, the telephone bank First Direct asked in its advertising campaign 'What's next?' The slogan touched a raw nerve. Once you've led a revolution, once you've pioneered telephone banking, what *do* you do next? The obvious answer is internet banking, but First Direct's technology was not yet ready. Arguably, being single-minded about telephone banking made First Direct slow to exploit internet banking.

Its challenge is to unpack its big idea: to use it to generate entirely new services. And already one revolutionary service is under way, called Octopus. For a monthly subscription, Octopus answers customers' questions – on anything at all – over the phone. It's a new way of living the big idea – of sorting out complicated things for people in a fast and friendly way. It takes First Direct from banking into a wider arena it calls life management.

In a different world, Andersen Consulting began its second decade with some similar issues. It had created a hugely successful management consultancy with a particular strength in IT. And it had prevented dilution by establishing a powerful internal culture. It recruited exactly those people who would strengthen the mix. Through rigorous training programmes at its campus outside Chicago, it had built a formidable cadre of highly intelligent and highly ambitious consultants, located around the world.

But this single-mindedness produced weaknesses too. The firm needed to recruit more experienced people, but these new recruits found it hard to fit into the culture. It was highly American in feel, and needed a more diverse culture in order to grow worldwide. It was seen as a technology specialist, but the big money was in more strategic management consultancy.

Andersen Consulting responded by redefining its big idea, into 'helping our clients shape their future', which shifted the emphasis from creating a shared culture to creating a shared purpose. And then things moved on again. The firm changed its name to Accenture, dropping the 'Consulting' altogether, and promoting new services like the provision of venture capital. In its second age, it is busy adding new dimensions to its service, under the umbrella of its big idea.

For some companies, the second age is an age that demands new products. Saturn, the innovative American car company, has successfully established new ways of making and selling cars. As its website proclaims, 'We think a company that treats employees and customers better will build cars that are better too.' Through its partnership with the UAW union, and its network of retailers, it has created, as it claims, 'a different kind of company'. But it's found it hard to produce the right products.

'The challenge we face is product,' admits Nancy Brown-Johnston, director of organizational development. 'We didn't stay fresh enough. We've got a different kind of company, now we need a different kind of car. The story is yet to come on Saturn.'

The product challenge often goes to the heart of an organization's original big idea. First Direct has to offer services through other channels than its home channel. In just the same way, Saturn has to learn to make relationships with customers – and it's a relationship company more than a car company – through new channels like the internet. 'We're taking on the challenge of the internet age,' says Nancy Brown-Johnston. 'We're excited about that opportunity. The challenge is how to deal with people through the internet and still make a relationship. We're in our infancy here.'

The second age is an age of unpacking, translating the idea into new services and new channels.

3. Grown up, but the world has moved on

In its third age, the organization has grown up – it's been around for perhaps twenty years. That's young for a person, but relatively old for an organization. Old enough for the world to have moved on. Organizations in the third age often find that what they thought was a radical big idea is no longer radical: everyone else has caught up. The irony is that, by promoting a radical idea, they've made it less radical: they have, in a sense, put themselves into the mainstream.

The big question in the third age is therefore: how can we stay ahead of the wave?

The British television network Channel 4 is a good example. When it started in the early 1980s, it championed the alternative, it stood up for minorities, and its natural audience was the university-educated, liberal-thinking middle class. But most of this no longer seems remarkable. Society is more tolerant, tastes more catholic, taboos less powerful. 'People are now better educated,' says Channel 4's chief executive, Michael Jackson. 'The majority of people are now middle-class. Some of our aspirational values have become the province of the BBC and ITV. It's harder for us to be different now.'

And this is partly the result of Channel 4 itself: 'Channel 4 has profoundly influenced the television world,' says Michael Jackson. Reformers often make themselves obsolete. So when the world catches up, what do you do? 'It doesn't invalidate the idea, it's just more difficult.'

Channel 4 still espouses its original remit – expressed in the bland language of public service as 'innovation, originality, diversity, distinctiveness'. But it's turned up the volume on all these words. Michael Jackson talks about experimentation, permissiveness, hedonism and ambition. 'Television used to be a small pond,' he says, 'and it was easy to create a significant ripple with a pebble. Competition has made it a raging sea; and if you toss a pebble in now it has no impact. We need to toss boulders.'

Channel 4 is living its third age by taking the core of its original big idea – difference – and pushing that core thought as far as it will go. Its programmes are still made by independent production companies, but no longer does it wait for these producers to come up with ideas: it pushes its agenda very hard. 'We now try to say much more explicitly to production companies what we want. We need programme suppliers who understand the programme culture, the big idea.' It's much more focused than the early days of Channel 4. 'We've changed a lot of people, processes and thinking over the last two years. It's been a bumpy ride.'

Channel 4 has responded by focusing more, and looks set to stay robustly alive. Other organizations, with equally big ideas, hit their third age with a much more painful thud, and may not survive.

The third age is an age of focus – going back to the core idea, and if necessary changing what you do to push that core idea as far as it will go.

4. Mid-life

Mid-life comes early to organizations with a big idea – often in their thirties. However good the big idea, they can run out of steam.

In this, their fourth age, the question they ask is: how do we use the idea to renew our energy?

This was the challenge faced by Apple in the late 1990s. A big company with a great brand, but with a rapidly dwindling share of the market, and no profits. Founder Steve Jobs returned as interim chief executive. Within a year or two, a new product, the iMac, appeared. Suddenly, it was America's most sought-after consumer product – its fastest-selling computer ever. Apple was back in profit. Its share price soared.

A triumph, you would think, of the big idea. Steve Jobs had brought back to Apple its original specialness. He'd enabled Apple to rediscover its soul. Apple was about making computing fun, special, fashionable, quirky, almost human. Apple was for freedom, against authoritarianism. For people, against geeks.

True. But the real significance of the iMac story is that Steve Jobs used the big idea to energize Apple's huge internal resources. The iMac couldn't have happened so quickly on 'big idea' alone. It also needed a big company behind it. Steve Jobs's genius was to rejuvenate Apple – to fill its fourth age with some of the excitement of a first age.

As he puts it: 'We're trying to use the swiftness and creativity of a younger-style company, and yet bring to bear the tremendous resources of a company the size of Apple to do large projects that you could never handle as a start-up. A start-up could never do the new iMac. Apple now has the management and systems in place to get things like that done. I can't emphasize how rare that is. That's what makes Sony and Disney so special.'

The fourth age is about using the big idea in order to find new energy.

5. An over-familiar face

Any organization that reaches the fifth age is doing well. It has concentrated. It has unpacked its idea. As the world has changed, it has kept ahead. As it's grown older, it has stayed young. But because its idea is a social property, it's become rather a familiar face. Its people – employees and customers – know it, and know what it will do next. It just could get boring.

The question in the fifth age is therefore a profound one: how do we live the idea in completely new ways?

This question comes naturally to an organization like Virgin, which has instinctively questioned what it does all the way through its life. Virgin is now shifting its centre of gravity away from music and airlines, into finances and the internet. In the years ahead, it will therefore live its idea in (almost) completely new ways. The most tangible Virgin thing won't be a record shop or an aircraft, but a third-generation mobile phone, linked to the internet, through which people will organize their financial lives (and perhaps their other lives too). Virgin will still be about iconoclasm, but in a new arena.

IKEA, too, is asking the same question: how do we live the idea of 'democratizing design' in completely new ways? The world is getting used to IKEA stores – though it's certainly not getting tired of them. But couldn't there also be, for instance, IKEA schools, teaching people how to design their homes, or even how to run their own design businesses?

Even an organization that lives in a quieter pool – such as the British conservation charity, the Landmark Trust – knows it must rethink. The Landmark Trust, founded by Sir John Smith in 1965, rescues historic buildings, and then lets them out as holiday cottages. Already, you can book Landmark Trust holidays through affiliated websites, such as that of the John Lewis supermarket chain, Waitrose. But that's a detail. The real questions go deeper. 'Our head office', says its director, Peter Pearce, 'is in Sir John Smith's garden. We live two hundred yards from our founder. Our challenge is to keep the idea from the founder intact – but also to keep it relevant.' Peter Pearce actively looks for new employees who'll keep things moving. 'In recruiting,' he says, 'we look for a degree of eccentricity that you just can't manufacture. We want to find people who will not just take on the idea but take it forward.'

Not just taking it on, but taking it forward, and taking it into new worlds. It remains to be seen how an organization like the Landmark Trust will do that, though its big idea – 'experiences of a mildly elevating kind' – is big enough to suggest all sorts of possibilities.

And many of today's biggest big ideas open up vistas of opportunity. Think what Aveda could do with 'purity', outside the arena of cosmetics. Or how Fannie Mae could develop the idea of 'home-ownership'. Or what GE could do to promote its big idea, 'learning'. Or how Nokia could find new ways to be 'future leaning'.

The fifth age is, or should be, an age of new dimensions.

6. Against orthodoxy

The sixth age of a big idea is a time of high maturity. Organizations that reach this age have attained real stature in their world, whether they're Bang & Olufsen or the BBC, Shiseido or Shell, Disney or McKinsey. They've been around long enough to have a very strong sense of themselves, and people in all of these organizations will talk passionately (and argue passionately with colleagues) about what their organization does, and doesn't, stand for. And they're recognized as citizens of their worlds: some of them are seen as members of the establishment.

The enemy, in this age, is orthodoxy. Orthodoxy in two senses. First, big ideas, as they grow older, can turn to dogma. They can become an unthinking orthodoxy within the organization. They become the answer, not the question. Second, a big idea can become part of the orthodoxy of the society it operates in. It can lose its radical, nonconformist edge. The organization, as a result, no longer stands out, because it no longer stands for something distinctive.

So the question in the sixth age is: how can we fight orthodoxy?

Sir John Browne, at BP, is fighting orthodoxy with a highly challenging big idea, 'Beyond Petroleum'. He wants to build an enterprise that – while still producing oil – doesn't think like an oil company. Some green campaigners expect BP to pull out of hydrocarbons altogether. No, responds Sir John: 'Beyond Petroleum just means that we are giving up the old mindset, the old thinking that oil companies had to be dirty, secretive and arrogant.'

The key word is 'beyond': Sir John's thinking wants

to move the company beyond current convention, beyond current conflicts. And below the big idea is a set of medium-sized ideas he calls key strands. 'They're a mix of values and policies. Things you hold firm. And that have an edge to them – that you can measure.'

BP's key strands include the environment. 'People say either you believe in a clean environment or you believe in burning hydrocarbons – we say we can do both.' They include the idea of well-being. 'People think there's a trade-off between a company's success and individual well-being – that commercial success means working ever longer hours, for example – that's a false trade-off.' Another, as we've already seen, is scale. 'However big you are, you also have to be very small, so people feel ownership. We have 150 business units – so in each unit you can almost get everybody into one room.'

For BP, these ideas are solid but not immovable. 'You have to be open to new ideas, and, if they have a place, they have to change what you do,' insists Sir John. Their huge benefit to BP is that they create a *feel* for where the business needs to go. Through them, managers can make strategic and tactical decisions that help secure the company's future, without being hamstrung by huge, weighty strategic plans that are out-of-date the moment they're printed.

There's a link between these medium-sized ideas: they're all to do with the bringing together of opposites, or as Browne likes to say, 'transcending trade-offs'. The idea that you can have the economic benefits of oil and gas *and* protect the environment. The idea that you can have the advantages of being small (through small business units) *and* of being large (by networking them together). The idea that you can have a tough, performance-driven workplace *and* a decent quality of life: that you don't have to start work at 6 am in order to succeed.

In every case, the aim is to move beyond current thinking, to thwart orthodoxy, and so to survive in the sixth age.

Other organizations tackle the question of orthodoxy in different ways. Rajat Gupta, senior partner at McKinsey, admits that 'We do need to modernize our values from time to time.' But he's confident that this will happen anyway, that the spirit of dissent is alive and well. 'If you were a fly on the wall in a partner meeting,' he says, 'you'd be surprised. We're always challenging, questioning – there's always an ability to dissent.'

And other organizations, like the BBC, have an inbuilt resistance to internal orthodoxy. A management orthodoxy planted by former director general Sir John Birt (and heavily influenced by McKinsey) didn't take firm root, and is being tugged out by his successor, Greg Dyke.

Others stoutly maintain their orthodoxy, but allow dissent at the edges. The John Lewis Partnership is very clear about right and wrong. 'You don't have a grey, you have a black-and-white company,' says chairman Sir Stuart Hampson, rather terrifyingly. But the company's staff journal, the *Gazette*, allows a quite extraordinary degree of steam to be vented. In one recent issue, a reader challenges the chairman's salary, and another accuses the company's supermarket, Waitrose, of overcharging. These letters aren't censored – though, significantly, they're signed pseudonymously.

The Japanese cosmetics company Shiseido tests orthodoxy through an annual questionnaire, in which it asks

5000 representatives of all its stakeholder groups to assess how well it's achieving its big idea. 'We use it to identify new stakeholder demands,' says chairman Akira Gemma. 'This information is shared amongst all management and staff. For example, board directors have an overnight meeting where they refine and improve the guidelines for our corporate activities.' He adds: 'Whenever there are any significant changes in what each stakeholder demands, we will change accordingly. We must not be rigid in the face of change.'

In these and other ways, organizations can discourage orthodox thinking inside. But a bigger danger may be the outside view – the danger of being *seen as* orthodox.

The BBC, BP and John Lewis are all part of the British establishment – that's why their leaders' names start with 'Sir'. Equally, McKinsey is part of the world business establishment. Even Tesco – which chirpily 'likes its customers' and cheekily challenges the law on 'grey market' imports – now supplies Christmas puddings to the British royal family.

This is a strength: it helps them win people's trust. For the biggest news events, for instance, people almost automatically choose to watch the BBC.

But it's a weakness too, and a growing one. Being orthodox makes you part of the background, not the foreground. An organization that's part of the establishment is eminently safe but not very exciting. It has lost the edge, the nonconformism, the radicalism – the anger, almost – that makes people want to give it their time, money and energy. And this becomes more of a problem when you remember the consumer's new search for authenticity, and the employee's search for something to identify with, and the investor's search for future value. The safe, mainstream, conformist organization can easily seem inauthentic – it's given up its search for the real, the different, the hand-made, the awkward, the challenging. It can be much harder for an increasingly nonconformist workforce to believe in. And for both those reasons it can become an eminently worthy source of *past* value, but a questionable source of *future* value.

The sixth age is a comfortable age that tries to get less comfortable, in order to avoid the dangers of orthodoxy. It's an age of dissent.

7. Culture shock

Organizations in the seventh age are, by any standard, venerable. With their longstanding big idea, they have a firm place in the hearts of millions of people. And they're driven, day to day, by a distinctive and resilient culture.

But their strength is also their weakness. For these organizations, culture is the enemy. Culture is a barnacle that grows round a big idea, and eventually slows down the whole organizational ship. Culture is often defined as 'the way we do things around here', and it's dangerous for organizations to keep doing things, year after year, in the same way. Strong cultures can be risky things.

The question in the seventh age, therefore, is: how can we scrape away at the culture?

The answer is: read the outside world. Watch how the world is changing, and in the light of that change, find new interpretations of the big idea. Don't, whatever you do, scrap the big idea. But reorient it. Like a diamond, twist it round so that new facets become visible.

Most leaders of seventh-age organizations can recall times of slumber, times when this kind of alertness to the outside world wasn't happening, and when the culture, by default, took control.

The National Trust, for instance, has seen decades of fast progress, and decades where, with hindsight, it seems to have been becalmed. 'When the Trust hasn't been alert,' says Martin Drury, 'it has slowed down. This happened in the 1920s and 30s, for example. But then we became alert to the need to rescue country houses in the 1940s. Gardens were the big thing in the 1950s. And smaller and modern buildings in the 1980s and 1990s.'

He believes that it's a large part of his job to encourage – to demand – alertness. The Trust's new issue this decade is the environment. 'We know that the big preoccupation of our members and staff will be environmental issues – research has revealed this. We will have to take up positions on these issues. We have to stay alert to people's interests, even ahead of them.'

Martin Drury recognizes that things inside the organization don't always change as fast as these external preoccupations: 'internally, the systems change more slowly'. Culture inevitably exerts its drag. But you can scrape away, by getting people to re-examine the big idea. 'We've recently carried out a purpose and values project,' he says, 'whose aim was to devise a contemporary interpretation of the Trust's purposes.' Reinterpretation, not reinvention. 'The trick is to keep faith with the simple and noble purpose of our founders, while responding to the concerns of the day.'

Reinterpretation is the word at the *Guardian* newspaper too. In its 170 years, the newspaper has seen times of growth and times of stagnation. 'A big idea', says its editor, Alan Rusbridger, 'can lead to self-satisfaction, smugness. It happened to the *Guardian* in the 1980s. A new rival, the *Independent*, came along and read the political and cultural world better. As a result the *Guardian* circulation went into a nosedive.'

How to guard against that complacency? 'Each editor has to reinterpret the big idea for their generation,' says Alan Rusbridger. Each editor has to read the political and cultural world, and change things accordingly. 'It's about enough new blood coming in. I see part of my job as making life uncomfortable for staff as well as comfortable. That's very difficult to manage internally, since there's a lot of people in their fifties who still have a lot to give.'

The dual task is to reinterpret the big idea, and to disrupt the culture – to make things constructively uncomfortable. The real trick is to bring these two tasks together: to use the big idea to *question* the prevailing culture.

At the moment the internet is adding extra complexity to this task. Every organization needs some internet experts. These people have their own culture – there's an internet language, an internet way of doing things. So when you create an e-business unit, you are bringing a second influential culture into your organization. The risk is that you end up with two organizations, the old and the new, pulling in different directions. For Alan Rusbridger, there's also a physical gulf – the original *Guardian* and its electronic offspring are based in different buildings, on opposite sides of the road.

'We've got eighty people working over the road on the online edition,' he says. 'How do you get them inculcated in the *Guardian* big idea? They understand the ethos of the web but not of the *Guardian* – and a lot of people in this building think the online version is nothing to do with the *Guardian*.' Alan Rusbridger's problem is replicated in almost every organization at the moment. And the best solution is to use the big idea to question both the old and the new culture. If the *Guardian*'s big idea is 'outsider', then how does an outsider put together a newspaper? And how does an outsider exploit the internet?

Several venerable seventh-age organizations have built their prosperity on the big idea of integrity. Integrity has been the core of their culture. They're now finding that their culture has slowed them down, that younger rivals can move faster, and that they need to reinterpret integrity for a new century.

'Over the past one hundred years,' says Ratan Tata, chairman of India's biggest firm, 'Tata has stood for fair play, good value for money, justice for the customer.' In an often murky commercial world, Tata's insistence on integrity was a radical departure, and the firm stood out as a beacon. But it was an unusual marketplace. 'We offered good products, but often they were the only product. In many of the fields in which we operated, we had no effective competition.' And now that has changed. 'Today we may not always have the best product, but our image is ahead of our products in several areas.' In other words, Tata's reputation for integrity is greater than the true value of some of its products.

Tata is therefore swivelling round its big idea. Now, 'justice for the customer' demands a more energetic, less complacent culture. Better products, produced much more efficiently. 'We need to stand for leanness and nimbleness,' he says. 'The goal used to be to produce as much as we could, because we could sell it all. But tomorrow's Tata will need to be much leaner, more goal-driven.'

How do you change culture in such a large and diversified corporation, across such a huge country? 'Obviously we need fresh blood. The first task is to get new blood on board.' But there's a catch-22 here: 'The best potential recruits are concerned that, if they come to Tata, they'll be swamped in the present culture.' The way forward is to use the big idea – about integrity to the customer – to question the old culture, and to attract the right kind of new people.

Britain's Marks & Spencer similarly grew big through integrity, but was then slowed down dramatically by its culture.

The original idea behind Marks & Spencer was about a new kind of honest trading. Quality was good, prices fair. Over time, the idea acquired new dimensions – that goods would be made in Britain, that the company wouldn't advertise, that if you didn't like something you'd bought, you could always bring it back. Every member of staff received a non-contributory pension, and Marks & Spencer was one of the biggest charity givers in the country.

The Marks & Spencer big idea was a complex mix, adding up to a certain kind of integrity perhaps best expressed as respectability. Marks & Spencer was respectable, and shopping there made its customers respectable.

Around that idea grew a culture. And that culture made it hard for M&S to see that there might be other, better ways of doing things. When it tried to catch up with rivals on customer service, it couldn't help doing it in its own stilted, bureaucratic way. When other supermarkets offered, for instance, to 'replace and refund' goods that customers were unhappy with, M&S copied. But its posters were headed 'Foods refund policy', and worded like an internal memo.

In 1998, after a public boardroom battle, and an autumn of disastrous trading figures, the media turned against their former idol, and in just a few months, people – customers and employees – stopped believing in the big idea. With all its dirty washing aired in public, the company no longer seemed particularly respectable.

But Marks & Spencer, like most seventh-age businesses, is strong enough to survive. Integrity – honest trading – is a big enough big idea. It just needs reinterpretation, in a way that undermines the old autocratic culture of 'closing ranks'. One option – and the company is already doing a lot in this area – is to be the retailer that's best at organic foods, at products free of genetically-modified ingredients, at ensuring fair wages for its third-world clothing workers, at reducing unnecessary packaging, at cutting the energy its stores use up, and so on. This, after all, is the new respectability: and it's ideal territory for Marks & Spencer.

The seventh age is an age of reorientation: reinterpreting the big idea in a way that questions the culture.

The special energy

In theory these are the seven ages of a big idea. But reality, of course, is never as neat as this.

Some organizations move through the ages much faster than others. Some skip a stage. Some, maybe, go backwards.

In your organization, you may be able to detect the symptoms of several different ages, all at the same time. You may, for instance, be sagging in energy (the fourth age) and growing the barnacles of culture (the seventh age) – and yet be only a few years old. You may have bought, or been bought by, another organization, and this may have confused everything. Reality is messy.

But the overriding principles still apply. The best organizations use their big idea to question things, not to answer them. In their early years, they keep their idea as concentrated as possible, and use it to suggest as many new products and services as possible. In their later years, they use it to undermine orthodoxy and to unsettle their culture, aiming to find new worlds to enter, or radical new interpretations of the radical old idea.

Organizations with a big idea never get there. They never arrive. There's always more to do. That's the source of their special energy.

CHAPTER NINE

all the difference

What difference does a big idea make? Isn't it just an optional extra, a fashion accessory? Cute, but in the end trivial?

It's true that the world is full of large, successful organizations that patently don't have a big idea. But a big idea is starting to make a difference. And soon, it may make *all the difference*.

A big idea makes a difference to profit. John Lewis achieves a profit per square foot of £503, compared with £210 for rivals Debenhams and £194 for House of Fraser. And this kind of business advantage can be just as useful to a non-profit organization – a big idea can make it easier and cheaper to attract the right kinds of funding.

But a big idea affects more than just today's profits. It also gives an organization a much more secure place in the future. It can't guarantee a future, but it can certainly help get an organization through hard times, and enable it to move swiftly to wherever the best opportunities lie.

This kind of future security makes a big difference to today's value. France Telecom paid £27 billion for Orange. A majority of the world's ten most valuable organizations, measured by their market capitalization, have some kind of big idea. For them, a big idea has helped create a big valuation.

Finally, a big idea makes another kind of difference. Beyond profit, beyond market capitalization, it makes the world a better place.

High ground

A big idea gives an organization the high ground. In the marketplace, the idea stands out like a beacon, attracting new customers and new employees – often without the need for expensive advertising. Inside the organization, the idea steers everyone's decision-making: there's no need for an unwieldy structure of command and control, or a vast bureaucracy.

And that's how a big idea makes an organization more profitable: it becomes more visible, more attractive and more single-minded, at a lower cost.

The idea of 'home-ownership', for example, has done that for Fannie Mae, creating over the last thirty years one of the world's largest financial services corporations, with double-digit profits growth.

A big idea is like a hill-town – a stronghold, a focal point, something that people can orientate themselves by, while the cities on the plain fight it out below. To start with, a big idea gets an organization noticed. We live in a cacophony of indistinct marketing noise. We're surrounded by blurred messages. Anything strong and pure will stand out. And if it's simple, it becomes memorable.

That's how big corporations like Disney and Coca-Cola have stood out for decades. And it's how newer businesses like Ben & Jerry's or Amazon or IKEA or Virgin have made their mark. A big, simple, strong idea gives anyone a huge advantage in a world of cacophony: you get noticed, and you get remembered.

It's also the reason why branded-goods makers are drastically cutting the number of brand names they use – in Unilever's case, from 1600 down to 400.

And it's not just commercial corporations that need the high ground of public attention. Amid a million good causes, non-profits like Greenpeace or Amnesty International have built their influence on the foundations of a strong and simple idea. Government programmes, such as Britain's welfare-to-work programme, equally need to be heard. 'A new policy needs to inspire people,' says treasury minister Andrew Smith. 'In an information-rich world, with an unprecedented array of signals and messages, people need a feeling as well as a mental image. With our New Deal programme, that feeling – that big idea – is "hope".'

Because big ideas have this emotional component, they do more than attract attention: they encourage desire. People really *want* Sony televisions, they're *determined* to stay at a Mandarin Oriental, they *can't wait* to get to Disneyland, they *love* their iMac.

The emotions and feelings associated with a product 'can make it stand out from the crowd', says strategy expert Michael De Kare-Silver. 'They can be compelling. They can create desire. They can persuade the customer to choose a particular product even when all other things between it and its rivals – performance, service and price – are seen as equal.'

And that's the point: big ideas help people buy things. For non-profits, they help people become donors, funders, supporters. For an organization without a big idea, life is harder. It may be noticed, it may be tolerated, it may even be admired, but it's not loved. It doesn't draw people in. People don't simply buy. Instead, it has to spend money and energy on selling, selling, selling.

And a big idea attracts not just any customers, but the right ones. McKinsey's insistence on its idea of 'rigour' attracts only the most serious clients: those most likely to commit to a substantial, long-term working relationship. First Direct's idea was designed to appeal to relatively upmarket, self-assured people who wanted to vent their frustrations with traditional banking – which meant that it brought in a distinctive group of new customers, rather than simply taking accounts from its parent, HSBC. And Orange's idea attracts customers prepared to spend more: Orange's revenue per user was £483 in 1998, compared with a mere £280 for rival One-2-One.

What's more, if a big idea creates a burning desire among high-spending customers, then it opens the door to higher prices. Because relatively rich people get particularly excited about 'experiences of a mildly elevating kind', the Landmark Trust can charge a great deal more than the average holiday cottage company. The new VW Beetle attracts a premium price: people really desire that unique mix of obsession with detail and quirkiness. Because people get passionate about 'poetry', they'll pay more for Bang & Olufsen. McKinsey charges top-drawer fees for its top-drawer rigour: indeed, charging less would undermine the credibility of its big idea.

Of course, not every organization with a big idea charges higher prices. Some, like Go and Tesco, trade lower prices for a longer relationship.

Big ideas, then, bring in customers. They also make customers want to stay. If an idea is big, true and substantial, then it's not mere fashion, and people will continue to believe it. Of the British mobile phone networks, Orange has by far the lowest 'churn': its customers stay with it.

This staying power goes much deeper than the 'loyalty' created by discount cards. 'We've never had a loyalty card,' says Sir Stuart Hampson of John Lewis. 'The genuine loyalty of John Lewis and Waitrose customers far exceeds the promiscuity of people with a walletful of store cards – which isn't loyalty at all.'

It's not only deeper, it's also cheaper. 'As many as 92 per cent of our customers say they'd fly Go again,' says Barbara Cassani. But that's because they like Go, not because they're collecting frequent flyer miles. 'In fact, we can't afford frequent flyer programmes.'

And this is a consistent pattern among organizations with a big idea. They manage to win customers – the right customers – and to keep them, without spending billions on loyalty schemes or on advertising. A big idea works better than both.

Marks & Spencer – through all its years of growth – hardly advertised at all. John Lewis rarely runs advertising, compared with its department store rivals. In its early years, Virgin Atlantic spent 2 per cent of turnover on advertising, well below the 5 to 7 per cent industry norm.

Instead, big ideas generate free advertising. They provide juicy content for journalists, and so encourage positive coverage in the media. And they are the lifeblood for word-of-mouth recommendations. These two vectors both carry the huge advantage over advertising that they look independent and unbiased.

The more a big idea is radical and controversial, the more media attention it gets. It's particularly helpful to play

David, fighting an industry Goliath, as both Virgin and Ben & Jerry's have found.

And the more an idea is tangible – the more that customers can *feel* it – the more effect the organization gets from word-of-mouth recommendation. 'We benefit hugely from the free advertising done by our early adopters,' says Alun Thomas of Heathrow Express. 'Without the big idea, people would still use us, but we wouldn't get the 98 per cent we currently get who say they'll recommend us. It's the extra things that get you affection and loyalty.' Similarly, 80 per cent of First Direct customers say they'd recommend the bank to friends. And 95 per cent of Saturn buyers, according to Tom Peters, 'urge others to join their club'.

That's the power of a big idea: customers who are not only committed themselves, but act as advocates to others. Even those organizations who choose to spend heavily on advertising – Tesco, Gap, Orange, Sony – benefit from this effect: customer advocates multiply the impact of every pound or dollar or yen they invest.

But a big idea can do more. Not only can it cut the cost of selling, it can also cut the cost of managing. And it does that in much the same way: by acting as a beacon.

Any organization is full of Brownian motion: tens or hundreds or thousands of employees each doing what they think is right, but each going in a slightly different direction. It's wasteful, counter-productive, expensive. A big idea reduces that costly randomness.

It unites people, and so cuts friction. John Lewis's big idea, says Sir Stuart Hampson, 'removes so much of the friction of a conventional business'.

It creates a mood, a personality, that's much more effective than any elaborate strategic plan – which probably cost millions to put together and is already out of date. As Sir John Browne of BP says, 'Strategy is not about setting a single-point direction, it's more about establishing a personality.' That's what a big idea can do.

It provides some simple rules that work better than any corporate manual could possibly do. 'We've tried to run Tesco by remote control, formats, procedures,' says chief executive Terry Leahy. 'It's very tempting in retailing. But however sophisticated your systems, you can't have an instant answer to everything. People have to understand a common set of values, so that their reaction is your reaction.' Leahy looks at his watch. 'At this moment,' he says, 'if our store manager in Korea has the right checkout service on, it's because he knows the Tesco values, not because he's following procedure number 399.'

The mention of Korea is significant. As organizations grow around the world, it becomes harder and harder to keep things together. The forces are all centrifugal. Whether an organization grows organically or by acquisition, the same thing happens. New people join who want to do things their way: 'the way they're done here', or 'the way we've always done them'. The chief executive is up against the massed forces of geography and history.

These forces are friendly when they encourage people to be sensitive to local markets, or when they unleash local enthusiasm and energy. But they're dangerous when they make the organization look fragmented to customers, or when they discourage collaboration among employees.

A big idea can help. Disney's idea about 'fun' enables it to keep an extraordinary range of activities and places together – from a cable channel in New York to a store in Johannesburg to a theme park in Tokyo.

A big idea makes it all instinctive and natural. It's management by instinct not rulebook, atmosphere not bureaucracy, personality not plan.

This style of management encourages employees to do their best, and to stay. *Fortune* quoted an employee of Southwest Airlines: 'Working here is a truly unbelievable experience. They treat you with respect, pay you well, and empower you. They use your ideas to solve problems. They encourage you to be yourself. I love working here!'

Of course, there are drawbacks too. Because people in this kind of organization feel so strongly about things, passions can run high. 'Life at the National Trust', says Martin Drury, 'is both stimulating and volatile. There's a huge amount of personal ownership of the purposes, which means that people are sometimes frustrated, disappointed.' Everyone thinks their part of the organization matters most, and most deserves attention and investment.

In many organizations with a big idea, there are no clear rules, and no comfortable culture. Michael Jackson at Channel 4 contrasts life there with the BBC: 'The corporatist, corridor culture of big organizations like the BBC can be good at having a culture, at training people, at a sense of belonging – I've moved from corporate certainty to decentralized uncertainty.'

Managing by ideas, by values, by talking and listening can appear worryingly unstructured to more conventional managerial minds. As Bang & Olufsen's Anders Knutsen says: 'It's hard to explain that values-based management is more about raising questions than giving answers – and my board is concerned sometimes that I'm becoming too philosophical.'

Above all, a big idea creates very high expectations. 'It

makes life more difficult for us,' says Hans Snook at Orange. 'The downside is we increase people's expectations. Children know if someone they trust lies to them: it's very destructive of the psyche of that child.' An organization with a big idea earns the trust of customers, employees, investors, the media. One tiny mistake can destroy that trust. Organizations who seem to be denying their big idea attract overwhelmingly negative media coverage. Because their big idea was a social property – deep inside the hearts of thousands of people – their failings can evoke a deep and widespread anger. An organization that has attained the high ground, but then loses people's trust, has a long way to fall.

But that's the nature of high ground.

A place in the future

Because a big idea gives an organization the high ground, it makes for bigger profits. But it does more than that: it also carves out space into the future. It makes it much more likely that the organization will be where it wants to be next year, and five years from now, and ten years from now. And because an organization's value depends on its future prospects, a big idea makes for a higher value.

How does a big idea stake out this kind of future space?

To start with, it makes a space that rivals can't invade. A big idea is a unique property. Because it's the soul of the organization, it's the one thing that others can't copy.

When virtually everything else can be bought or stolen, matched or copied, this matters. As everyone knows, clever processes, smart new product ideas, even whole business models are up for grabs. At the moment, almost everyone can get the capital they need. An organization's people, of course, make a huge difference – but they can be persuaded to walk. The strange and nebulous – but always recognizable – thing called a big idea is the only thing an organization can be sure to hold on to.

No one else can purvey Virgin's idea of iconoclasm. Of course, others can use the word, but no one can do it Virgin's way. Anyone who adopted Virgin's consumer's-champion attitude and its laid-back style would simply look like a cynical copy. It might work for a while, but it could never steal Virgin's high ground. Similarly, no one else can take Aveda's idea of purity, or Muji's idea of the no-brand brand.

Even if someone tries to emulate a big idea, there's one thing they can never be: first. Someone else got there first, staked out the ground, claimed ownership of the idea. They are authentic, they are the real thing. And in a marketplace that increasingly values authenticity, that makes a big difference.

Of course, no one's future is certain. But without a big idea, the prospects are chillier. Anyone could replicate your business, or copy your charity. Maybe they already have.

And given that futures are never certain, a big idea has another useful effect. Whatever setbacks await the organization, a big idea can help it survive.

Apple bounced back into profit by making a product, the iMac, that brought its original big idea back to life. Here was a computer that, like the very first Macintosh, overturned everyone's expectations of what a computer is like. It was easy to use, and – even more important – it was lovable. Apple's big idea had given it two kinds of resilience. First, through a number of difficult years, its original way of thinking stayed alive inside the organization, and enabled it eventually to produce the iMac. Second, the idea continued to burn away in the minds of customers. Enough of them stayed committed to Apple through the hard times, and plenty of them came back when they recognized the qualities of the iMac. Without its big idea, it's doubtful whether Apple would have survived. In practice, Apple turned a billion-dollar loss in 1997 into a $600 million profit two years later.

In a similar way, Bang & Olufsen weathered a prolonged storm in the early 1990s. Indeed, B&O's big idea has given it remarkable resilience: since 1925, over a thousand European hi-fi companies have disappeared, and only B&O has survived.

The *Guardian* newspaper came under threat in the early 1990s, when its rival, *The Times*, started a price war. But the Guardian stood for something. And that enabled it to stand firm, and not to cut its price. 'The corporate idea enabled us to maintain our cover price,' says editor Alan Rusbridger. 'Without that, if we'd pursued *The Times* into cost-cutting, we'd have been sunk.'

This in-built resilience matters even more for non-profits, particularly small ones whose continued existence hangs on little more than the enthusiasm of staff and supporters. 'Without a big idea,' says Peter Pearce, director of the Landmark Trust, 'we could still run a very capable historic buildings letting agency. But in hard times no one would care deeply if it went to the wall. Regular customers would drift away. Staff's sense of fulfilment – that it's not just a job – would suffer. There's a spirit about an organization like the Landmark – that's why I joined.'

A big idea gives an organization emotional territory it

can own. It gives it a special resilience in hard times. But most importantly of all, it gives it scope to grow.

The great thing about most big ideas is that they don't limit the organization to one narrow sphere of activity, or one parochial place on the globe.

Disney can do anything that's about fun. Orange, if it wanted to, could offer any service that was about optimism and freedom. The BBC can operate in any sphere where authority matters. Amazon can offer completeness in any field – not just books or music or auctions but absolutely anything.

So if one kind of activity gets tough, or goes out of fashion, none of these organizations is stuck. They hit a problem only if their *idea* becomes stale.

Without a big idea, an organization can soon reach its limits. Its core business may become cut-throat. Its formula may not work outside its home market. It may be unable to assimilate acquisitions, or to get bigger without fracturing.

But the right kind of idea makes all the difference.

The universality of IKEA's idea, for example, has taken it all around the world. The same is true for Coca-Cola, Gap, Tesco, Orange.

The determination of BP's idea is enabling it to assimilate acquisitions, without losing its magic.

And the ethical strength behind the venture capital firm 3i has enabled it to grow much bigger than most firms of its kind. 'No venture capital firm in the States has anything like the scale of 3i,' says chief executive Brian Larcombe. 'They get to about ten people, then have a big row over dividing up the money, and split off. Our ethical principle is the key to our scale.'

The power of a big idea to keep people together will

become yet more important in the future. Already we're seeing professional service giants starting to fracture. And, since more and more organizations are becoming rather like professional service firms – full of bright, independent-minded knowledge workers – these community break-downs will become more and more common. Organizations will need to build and maintain communities of people, both outside and inside the traditional organizational boundaries. For Alan Rusbridger at the *Guardian*, this is critical. 'Having readers you can draw on and tap into will be a very valuable thing for us – readers who can write reviews, contribute material, and form communities with other readers.' It may well be that the real limit to growth in the future will be an organization's ability to build cohesive communities – communities with a strong enough shared interest to make them last.

A big idea can make an uncertain future that bit more secure. It can hold back the competition. It can keep people committed. And it can fuel growth: new markets, new services, new and bigger communities of people.

Big idea, big value

In all these ways, a big idea gives an organization a space in the future. And a room reservation in the future is what makes an organization valued today.

The end of the twentieth century saw a quite extraordinary change in what is valued by the hard-nosed people who drive stock markets. Stock markets now recognize that there's much more to a business than those assets that accountants can touch and feel.

In 1988, for example, the proportion of the market capitalization of Britain's FTSE 350 companies represented by tangible assets was 56 per cent. Ten years later, it had declined to 29 per cent. This means that investors now place huge value on goodwill, brands, culture, management style, intellectual property – on what's in the heads and hearts of an organization's employees and customers. And this isn't a modest revaluation: it's a fundamental rethink by investors. Of every pound invested in a big British company, 71p now represents that company's intangible assets.

Why such a radical rethink, by a notoriously conservative group of people? Because investors and analysts place value on what's rare. Tangibles – buildings, machinery, technology – are readily available. Capital is readily available. What's in short supply is the intangible. There's a limited supply of customer goodwill, of new product ideas, of brilliant management skills, of visions, of brands – and, increasingly, of the big idea that underlies and drives all of those things.

Accountants Ernst & Young have looked at how investment decisions are made. They've come back with an incongruously precise figure: 35 per cent of any investment decision, they say, is driven by non-financial data. Of this non-financial information, what matters most are measures of strategy execution, management credibility, innovation and market position. They single out quality of strategy: does management have a vision of the future? And it's the future that matters most here. In their dry accountancy language, they make the most crucial of points: 'Financial metrics are lagging indicators; proactive managers need to balance the focus on both the hard numbers and intangibles that will drive value in the future.'

Valuing a company used to be relatively simple. You looked at its recent history of profits and applied a multiple to get a price.

But now several of the world's most valuable companies have yet to make a profit. In theory, their market value should be zero. Why isn't it?

Because investors are interested in the future, not the past. They want to get as big a return as possible, for as long as possible. Until recently, past performance was a fair guide to future success. But in a fickle world, a star company can fall from the heavens, almost overnight. An institution as solid as Marks & Spencer can suddenly find that the world has moved on and left it behind.

Increasingly, investors want to find in a company a deep well of future profit. That means a piece of magic that will attract future customers, and enable them to be serviced at the lowest possible cost.

Many internet companies seem to investors to have this magic. In particular, they hold a lot of data about customers: terabytes of information on the people who visit their website – their buying patterns, their demographic secrets, their whole inner psychology of buying. This may be magic for a year or two: the trouble is, any reasonably successful e-business can build up a database of this sort.

In the longer term, the magic will be different. It will be a big idea – the sort of big idea that attracts tomorrow's consumer. This is the kind of idea every flotation, every initial public offering, will need. This will be the magic: this will be the well of future value.

It's therefore not surprising that, when you look at the world's most valuable businesses – those with the largest market capitalization – you find that most of them have a big idea.

Coca-Cola's cluster of ideas around 'the real thing' have created huge value out of a product that's not much more than sugared water. Plenty of other people sell the same thing – and sometimes, in blind tests, consumers prefer rival products – yet Coca-Cola staked first claim, and no one else can ever be 'the real thing'. And the big idea has taken Coca-Cola safely through very large-scale setbacks, like the disastrous introduction of a new formula in 1985, or problems with adulterated products in Belgium in 1999.

Microsoft's idea of 'ubiquity' has powered its extraordinary growth. It's true that the idea has more impact inside Microsoft than outside – and, indeed, that outside the company it can feel more like a threat than a promise. Nevertheless, the idea makes a powerful appeal to Microsoft's primary customers, the makers of personal computers – and to its primary partners, the suppliers of broadband communication networks.

GE is a collection of very different businesses – from generators to light bulbs, from finance to a television network – that are unified by an idea. Under Jack Welch's leadership, GE has created a real 'unity of feeling'. And that's made for an immensely valuable corporation. GE's idea – which is about learning – is currently more inspirational to insiders than to outsiders, and its challenge is to extend the idea into the outside world.

The same is true of Merck, with its idea about 'preserving and improving human life'. And Intel, with its quasi-scientific 'Moore's Law', about the speed with which computer technology improves. And Wal-Mart – an odd combination of folksiness and ruthlessness that's hard to put into words.

And, less surprisingly, the world's most valued non-profits also tend to have a big idea. There's no way of putting a market capitalization on non-profits, of course, but those that are most valued, most respected, most consulted by governments, would include Amnesty International, with its ideas around human rights, Greenpeace, with a very clear big idea about the environment, and the Red Cross, with its clear, clean, rather Swiss and yet very international idea about saving lives.

Interestingly, if you look at the world's *biggest* organizations, rather than the most valuable, the pattern doesn't hold. Most are long-established car-makers, oil companies, computer firms or (Japanese) conglomerates. Large-scale success in the twentieth century came from an ability to replicate efficient processes across traditional industries. A big idea was not needed.

But the new century is different. The new industries – pharmaceuticals, communications, consumer electronics, media, and the convergence of all these – are different. Any organization seeking value, rather than sheer size, needs to think differently. It needs something that's hard to copy and hard to resist. That thing is a big idea.

A better world

Big ideas do more than make profits and market capitalizations. At their best, they make the world a better place.

Throughout history, big ideas have inspired social and

scientific change. And in the modern era – the last two hundred years – that change has been delivered by organizations rather than by individuals. These organizations have always been a mix of the governmental (for example, the World Health Organization eliminating smallpox), the private non-profit (such as the abolitionist movement getting rid of slavery) and the commercial (for instance, Britain's Quaker businesses improving factory life in the nineteenth century). The pattern will continue. Many, perhaps most, organizations will continue to leave a neutral, or even a negative, legacy. But a few, with many different ownership structures, will continue to make things better.

No one's pretending that organizations with big ideas are perfect. Orange's customer service is far from perfect. John Lewis can sometimes seem dowdy and old-fashioned. The Body Shop has been accused of trading practices that fall short of its rhetoric. Some see EasyJet as just as attractive as Go. Disney has had a rocky time financially. Hewlett-Packard is accused of being worthy but dull. IKEA products are sometimes fiendishly hard to assemble. Some see the BBC as haughty, others accuse it of dumbing down. Saturn admits it has had problems getting its products right. And so on.

But all these organizations, and many others with a big idea, have made a difference, and continue to do so. The organizations that dominate our lives often seem to feed off us. It's particularly chilling to go inside an organization and find out how they talk about us, their customers: they talk about customer 'acquisition', 'retention' and even 'upgrade'. But instead of feeding off us, it's possible for organizations to nourish life, in a million different ways.

Some simply give pleasure. Mandarin Oriental hotels make staying in a strange city an enjoyable experience. Disney theme parks seduce even the most hardened sceptic into having fun. Southcorp makes wine with a wonderful depth of fruit flavour. These may be simple pleasures, but they're not simple to achieve. And a big idea fuels the hard, day-by-day commitment – the restless desire to do even better – that makes it all possible. A hotel without a big idea is merely a bed for the night. A wine made without passion is merely a drink. Big ideas do more.

Other organizations simplify life. In a world that conspires to make straightforward things into a struggle, they smooth it all out again. Instead of trekking round half a dozen bookshops in search of an elusive book, Amazon enables people to find it, read reviews of it – and order it with one click of the mouse-button. Most organizations just do a job – a train ride, a bookstore. Those with a big idea do more.

Organizations with a big idea make work more worthwhile. In many organizations, what matters most is the figures. Managers, in particular, find their lives dominated by spreadsheets. What matters is achieving the next quarter's forecast. It doesn't even matter whether the forecast is good. What's important is meeting it – regularity, predictability, certainty. And that's a reasonable way to run a business: many investors welcome consistency. But it makes for a disheartening work life. In other organizations, what matters is the customers, the product, the service, the underlying *idea*, whether explicit or unspoken. And for most people, that makes work worth doing.

Some organizations make life better by humanizing things. The twentieth-century's worship at the shrine of technology has left us feeling like supplicants to a harsh and unforgiving god. Anyone who's tried to programme a video recorder knows that. But some organizations have humanized technology. Apple made the computer a desirable, almost a cuddly, object. Bang & Olufsen squashed consumer electronics into seductive shapes that glamorize, rather than disfigure, living rooms. With the Walkman, Sony didn't just make a small tape player, it made the humdrum bits of people's lives – train journeys, waiting in queues – musical. And with the Playstation, Sony has tamed technology into toy. Many organizations construct clever objects: those with a big idea place them into human life.

Some organizations improve things simply by telling the truth. For decades, the BBC gave people living in totalitarian regimes a much more reliable account of the world than they could get at home. Management consultants McKinsey are committed to telling their clients the truth, whether it's welcome or not. Other media companies and other management consultancies don't set out to lie. But without a big idea, they're more likely to bend in the wind. As Reebok's Paul Fireman has put it: 'If you don't stand for something, you'll fall for anything.' A big idea gives an organization the steel to stand firm.

We live in a world dominated by mediocrity. Everywhere, people seem satisfied with second best. But organizations with a big idea *hate* mediocrity. People in them know by instinct that 'good' isn't good enough. Indeed, organizations with a big idea tend to suffer (and benefit) from endemic dissatisfaction with what they do, and a constant desire to do better. For its first thirty years, Penguin stood – with a few lapses – for the best in reading, not for whatever sells. IKEA stands for great design, not adequate design. If it makes a mistake, First Direct goes into overdrive to put things right: a mumbled apology isn't enough.

As well as keeping its own sights high, an organization with a big idea tends to raise the sights of its customers. It challenges and stretches people, by touching their emotions. Tesco introduced a huge range of new foods from around the world to the conservative British palate – not by simply putting them on to supermarket shelves and hoping for the best, but by creating an atmosphere in its stores which made people feel at home, and therefore feel comfortable about trying new things. Nike for years has challenged people to 'just do it', to go out and win.

Challenging us, stretching us, prodding us to do a bit more in our lives. Most organizations – who simply do what they do – can't achieve that. But organizations that offer not just *things* but a big *idea* can enlarge people's sense of themselves, can help them express themselves. Stores like Habitat and IKEA guide people's taste. They help them think harder about what they want their surroundings to look like, and therefore about what they want their surroundings to say about them, and therefore about who they are. Other stores simply provide furniture.

Perhaps most important of all, organizations with a big idea champion change. Big ideas are radical. They're not happy with the status quo.

They change whole industries for the better. Virgin has changed the airline industry for the better – and, more recently, the financial services industry too. It set new standards for in-flight entertainment, and championed good-value 'tracker' funds. Apple created a user-friendly computer operating system (designed originally by Xerox) and now every computer screen in the world has something very similar. Southcorp found clever new ways to make flavourful wine – and now even French wine growers are following suit.

Without big ideas, change would happen more slowly – gradual improvements, driven by gradually evolving customer demands, and slowed down by the ever-present force of consumer inertia. With big ideas, change is propelled by the passion of the organizations themselves, often moving years ahead of consumer expectations.

And sometimes they change more than just industries. IKEA likes to quote a Swedish politician who said that IKEA has meant more for the process of democratization than many political measures put together.

But these ways of improving the world may seem rather limited, rather materialistic. Is it really so great to have a better designed sofa, or a friendlier computer? Does it really matter to have a bit more fun in the world, a bit less complexity, a little more harmony, a little less deference? Are all these ideas really big?

Charles Handy talks about the people who built the medieval cathedrals, who collectively devoted three centuries to a building designed to glorify God. That, he suggests, is a big idea: a huge and pure aspiration.

And it's true, of course, that little is done these days for disinterested, transcendent, spiritual purposes, such as the glory of God. But in a secular age, plenty of non-profit organizations steadfastly pursue idealistic goals. And more and more businesses are discovering the need – while still making money – to be less narrowly interested in commercial goals. To be more concerned with issues that transcend day-to-day transactions. To be ready to touch people not just rationally, or even just emotionally, but to touch their spirits.

CHAPTER TEN

new business

What we've seen so far is just the beginning.

The beginning of a world in which organizations become communities. Whether it's a police force or an art gallery, an oil company or a bank, it's a community: customers, users, employees, volunteers, investors, trustees, suppliers, advisers, distributors networked together, electronically and emotionally.

This community is united not by *what* it does, but by *why* it does it, or by *how* it lives. It's united, in other words, by a big idea – about safe streets, or about seeing life through others' eyes, or about green energy, or about a better future, or about colour, or space, or nostalgia, or ingenuity, or whatever. It's a much less buttoned-down, looser, more colourful thing than the old-style organization, free to pursue new activities with a real zest for possibility and adventure. It has a sense of history and romance – but equally is sceptical of the false and the superficial.

It's a democratic community, where every member has real power – at a minimum, the power to leave that community – and may even have voting rights in determining its future. It's measured on its success in providing worthwhile returns to all its members, not just on profit or capital growth to its owners.

It's a community that may be tiny or huge, but where in either case there are more important goals than size. It may be worldwide, but it creates different experiences for different people in different places: all that matters is that each experience contributes to the big idea. It inspires unity among its members, but it also discourages homogeneity and conformity: sceptics and trouble-makers are welcome.

And it's a community run more on intuition than on science. Everyone in it recognizes the force of emotion: in making decisions, feeling matters as much as thinking. Inventing is seen as more valuable than compiling best practice. In thinking about its future, a naïve impulse may be just as valuable as a worldly-wise opinion.

Marx defined capitalism as a way that man relates to man. These communities offer a new kind of interrelationship: a new and better form of capitalism.

From organization to idea

We live in a frenzied world of 'what's next?' Consumers with new-found power and attitude are becoming increasingly impatient of the comfortable but bland world created by the twentieth century. People long not for consistency and certainty but unpredictability, looseness, possibility.

These people are pursuing a new goal: values for money. Consumers are looking to organizations to guide them, to offer them greater authenticity, and to behave ethically. People are excited not about how things could be, but how things *ought* to be.

And in this world, a new kind of organization is emerging. Whether it's commercial or non-profit, private or public, it's transforming itself from mere organization to a living community. In other words, it's less about organizing, more about communing. It's less concerned to regiment or compartmentalize its people, and more excited about letting them talk, compare notes, solve problems, get on with it. These organizations enable people to belong, without giving up any of their individuality. What unites their 'members' isn't stock options or the company culture or loyalty cards: it's that shared sense of how things ought to be.

In this new world, a few organizations have found a big idea: an idea that's full of that sense of 'ought'. It's radical – maybe even dangerously radical. It's social – all its members own it. And it's tangible: you can see, feel, touch it every time you encounter the organization, or interact with the community.

All the organizations in this book are there, or on the way. And in the next decade, we'll see more and more organizations like them. They will no longer be the exception. The traditional way we picture an organization has to change. It's not a factory or shop or hospital or school – it's not a building. It's not machinery, technology, raw materials – it's not things. It's not even a workforce, an organization chart, a 'customer base', a set of 'distribution channels' – it's not people. Buildings, things and people still matter, but they're not the heart, the core, the essence.

In the old model, the organization was the star. Customers revolved around the organization. The organization was there to secure its own survival. Now, it's different. The idea is the star. A community revolves around it. The goal is to make the idea a reality.

And, importantly, the idea belongs to the whole of that community. It's a social property. The community can develop it, reinterpret it over time. Indeed, all the exciting things happen *between* members of the community –

between employees on opposite sides of the globe, between customers, between customer and employee. The idea – the meaning of the community – is, in an important sense, out of control. The age of the control-freak organization is over. This is the stranger, less predictable but more exhilarating age of the community.

From market sector to emotional world

These big ideas are rare things. Gradually, the world's biggest ideas are being claimed.

So the most important marketplace is now the marketplace of ideas. The fight is on for the biggest and best.

And that fight will be very different from traditional competition. The new communities will compete – but they won't fight for market share within a traditional sector: they'll compete for what you might call heart-share within a particular emotional world.

Some, for instance, will contend within the emotional world of 'we're on the customer's side'. They'll fight for the biggest ideas on this theme. Others will compete in the emotional territory of integrity: they'll look for those kinds of integrity that resonate most powerfully in the new climate of the new economy. A third emotional world is the world of sensations – of sights, sounds, tastes and so on. Within this world, organizations will compete for the most exciting sensation-based ideas.

And there are many more emotional worlds – the new economy's version of the old idea of market sector.

From 'why?' to 'why not?'

The new organization is, in essence, an idea that inspires a community. That is its shape. But it has more than just a distinctive shape: it has a special kind of spirit too.

It's a spirit that says 'why not?' It believes that anything's possible, that categories are meaningless, that the market gives you permission to do anything.

Amnesty International, for instance, could sell pensions. IKEA could run schools. As long as it contributes to the big idea, any organization can do anything. The only limit is the organization's ability to acquire new capabilities – the skills to sell pensions or run schools. Yet even this limit isn't too demanding, in a world where anything can be outsourced.

All of this adds up to a new way of business. Not just commercial business, but a new way of living in any kind of organization. A way of living that's characterized not by the caution of 'why?' but by the exuberance of 'why not?'

And this spirit of 'why not?' is the real essence of that tarnished – but still important – thing, 'the new economy'.

The new economy isn't simply the internet or e-commerce or m-commerce (e-commerce conducted through mobile phones). That's just technology, a way of connecting people, a new channel for distributing things, a new kind of mail order.

Nor is it about high growth rates and low inflation rates, or a booming stockmarket. The graphs may soar, settle or plummet, but the spirit of 'why not?' will remain.

What matters isn't technology or economics. These things are signs of something more fundamental – of a desire to break free, to question assumptions, to make things better.

The internet is both a symptom and a cause of this desire. Its success – its amazingly rapid take-up among first Americans and then the rest of us – is a symptom of people's desire to find more things out, to experience more things, to buy things more easily (as well as their lazy wish to do all this without leaving their home). It conveniently enables people to do what they wanted to do anyway: to compare prices, find the best deal, compare experiences with other customers, make complaints direct to customer services staff by email. It enables, almost encourages, them to probe the affairs of any corporation for malpractice, and then to work up a campaign of protest. And it's also proof of people's readiness to forget old categories, to trust organizations they'd never heard of six months before, to say 'why not?'

Equally, of course, the internet redoubles all these desires: the more things become possible, the more excited people get about possibility. It's a cause as well as an effect.

Mobile phones, too, are both cause and symptom of a new spirit of freedom and possibility. Phone numbers now belong to people, not to places. You can be as accessible, or as private, as you want to be: you can, if you choose, be answerable to no one. People, like their phones, are mobile, on the move, unattached, free. Part of the genius of Orange was latching on to this spiritual dimension of mobile phones – showing people that a mobile phone could help them not just make a call, but join in a brighter future.

The internet and the mobile phone are symptom and cause of a spirit that wants to put the corporatist twentieth century behind us, to draw a line under the past, and to make something better.

In this climate, an organization is judged not so much on the services it offers, as on the way it offers them.

What matters in the new economy is the spirit in which organizations do things. Now, what you do matters much less than *how you are.*

From American to European

In some ways, this new spirit is a child of America. That's where entrepreneurs feel free to make their millions, in a heady 'can do' atmosphere. That's where the internet took off. That's where consumers are most ready to do battle with corporations, where a tradition of constitutional rights and ubiquitous litigation emboldens people to fight for their rights.

But in more important ways, this is a European spirit. It's a spirit of mobility, not just in the technological sense – and mobile phones took off much faster in Europe than in America – but in every sense of the word. Europeans travel frequently to each other's countries: nowhere is more than a few hours away. And increasingly, they can travel without a passport and carrying the same currency.

It's a spirit that comes from London and Paris and Rome and Berlin – but also, in interestingly different ways, from Copenhagen and Amsterdam, Helsinki and Stockholm, Madrid and Lisbon.

It's a way of business that's happy to embrace emotion and dream, community and story. It has a romantic tinge, and an historical tinge, which you rarely find in American business books.

This spirit grows out of a tradition in which commercial

organizations are more deeply embedded in society than they are in the American system: a tradition in which corporations own parts of each other in complicated webs of ownership, in which unions often have formal representation at board level, in which big companies employ, as a matter of course, doctors and social workers for their workers' families. This is a tradition that for decades has recognized that a corporation belongs to more than just its stockholders – that every stakeholder has a stake.

And before that, it's a tradition that goes back to the city-states of the Middle Ages, to the guilds, to the Hanseatic League – to all sorts of business communities.

But the spirit is also a reflection of the new European individual. We live within expanding boundaries: old national borders still exist, of course, but everyone is also a member of, or a close neighbour of, the larger – and still expanding – European Union. Expanding boundaries are part of the European way of thinking.

A large part of the emotional impetus behind this Union is the desire to draw a line under old, twentieth-century conflicts. A desire for new communities, rather than old confrontations.

But no one wants unity at the cost of uniformity. Europeans are every day aware of their linked but different cultures – either because they travel across borders, or because television and other media stray across borders into their homes. The value of 'linked but different' is close to European hearts.

Finally, and perhaps most importantly, there's a scepticism, a sense of perspective, that is in many ways European, and that is essential to this new spirit of business. It's the view that some things matter more than money. Free time, for instance: Europeans famously take far more holiday than Americans, and are far more protective of their non-work time. The environment, to take another example: Europeans started the campaign against genetically-modified ingredients.

Given a new business proposition, the American question has tended to be: 'Will it make money?' But a European might ask: 'What will it do for all of us?' In the new economy, the European question might just be the more searching one. Our model for the old corporation was fundamentally American: GM or Exxon-Mobil. Our model for the new community might be much more European: IKEA or Nokia or the Red Cross.

From your business to our business

The emotional ownership of organizations has already shifted. More and more, for any organization that concerns us, we feel that it's answerable to us. We feel that, in some sense, it's ours. We feel, to be precise, that *it's our business*.

It's a new kind of global village, in which everyone knows everyone else's business. From behind their net curtains – or internet curtains – someone's watching you. The anti-corporatist activists won't go away. Militant consumers are with us for good.

This makes the new way of business immensely refreshing. Complacency, carelessness and corruption will no longer go unnoticed or unpunished. Whatever an organization gets up to, someone will be watching. The new way of business is about challenge: customers challenging bad service, citizens challenging public agencies, organizations challenging their suppliers and partners. Those which rise to that challenge will survive. Those who don't – which continue to rely on the inertia of the marketplace – will find the ground opening beneath them, because the inertia of the marketplace is a fast disappearing phenomenon. People will no longer put up with bad performance just because they're used to it.

But it's about more than performance: it's about principle, too. Any organization must now be ethically impeccable – or be found out. And in the new way of business, principle isn't an extra, a luxury: it's a starting point. Social responsibility is not a differentiator: it's expected.

Organizations that donate to charity, that operate principles of fair trading in developing economies, that set themselves demanding environmental targets, are becoming not the exception but the norm.

So will all organizations become philanthropic foundations? Will every community operate for the greater good of mankind? No: life's not like that. The new way of business will be much more like the way, a hundred years ago, the Quakers in Britain ran their businesses.

The Cadburys, Rowntrees, Clarks and Barclays weren't fluffy-headed idealists: far from it. They were hard-headed business people, practical, methodical and orderly. They ran their companies to be effective businesses, not as charitable foundations. But everything they did was informed by a wider Quaker ideal: they sought to minimize conflict in the workplace, they developed high quality products and well-organized methods of recruitment and training, introduced profit-sharing and sick pay, and built decent housing for their factory workers. The Quakers created organizations

– communities – that naturally embodied the values of the wider Quaker community.

Similarly, the new way of business will be about organizations that are practical, efficient, business-like – but that are suffused with the values of the wider community, the community currently labelled 'the new economy'. These new businesses will, as a matter of course, behave ethically, encourage participation, recognize emotion, pursue beauty – because these are the values of the wider community they belong to. They will be *our business*.

From shareholder value to member value

In this global village, very little is private, very little can hide behind closed doors. Every organization – public or private, commercial or non-profit – is open to scrutiny. Secrets are now very hard to keep. Nothing is off-limits. Nothing is 'them'. We have every right, we feel, to probe sceptically – and to enjoy wholeheartedly.

This new way of business recognizes this emotional fact. It recognizes that power has shifted. No longer does one stakeholder group dominate the others. Instead, the organization emotionally belongs to everyone. The power therefore belongs to everyone. Every stakeholder matters. And the organization's idea must therefore inspire every stakeholder equally.

In the mid twentieth century, power in most large corporations lay with the managers. Often their nearest rival for power was organized labour – the trade unions – and sometimes the trade unions won. Either way, one stakeholder group or another came out on top. Then, in the

1980s and 1990s, the owners of corporations – the share-holders – reasserted their power. Shareholder value became the mantra, and companies downsized, divested, demerged in order to maximize their market value. Again, one stake-holder group dominated.

Now, it's all much more complicated. Employees can leave. Customers can boycott. Non-governmental organiza-tions can interfere. All are supported, or even led, by the media. The forces acting on an organization are much more complex, and much more finely balanced, than ever before.

In the new way of business, every organization has to inspire, and keep inspiring, its whole community. It's no longer enough to keep just one or two groups happy.

This thought isn't new, and many organizations have for years used management techniques designed to help them serve more masters than just their owners, to serve more aims than short-term profit. And techniques like the 'balanced scorecard' are certainly useful.

Yet the whole vocabulary of 'balanced' and 'scorecard' is starting to feel old-fashioned. The new way of business isn't about balance, it's about inspiration: it's not equilib-rium but dynamism. And it's not about ticking all the boxes on a scorecard, because inspiration can't be measured out in ticks or percentages.

How will the organization – the community – measure its success? This is a big new question for every kind of enterprise, from hospital to hotel, from mobile phone net-work to museum, from conservation charity to car manu-facturer. How can you assess the health of a community?

We'll see completely new ways of measuring emerge. What will count will be not 'shareholder value' but 'member value': the emotional value of a community to all its members. And these kinds of measure apply to every sort of organization, public and private, commercial and non-profit. For the first time, it will be possible to compare Greenpeace with Shell, or your local hospital with IKEA.

And what would 'member value' measure? The degree to which the community meets its members' expectations of ethical behaviour. The degree to which it allows them to participate, and to help shape the community's future. The degree to which members are able to communicate with each other, forming their own networks of people with shared interests. The extent to which members choose to stay members. The community's ability to plan its future, and fund those plans. The power of the community to inspire its members, and to keep inspiring them. Its success in managing its big idea over time – modulating it through the seven ages. And so on.

It's a different world of measurement: from earnings per share to inspiration per member.

From scale to beauty

At the end of the twentieth century, there was one thing you simply had to be: global. And that meant, for many organizations, that you had to be big. You had to have an office in every major city. You had to be everywhere. You had to have scale. In the new century, in the new way of business, global will still be important. But there will be something more important than scale: beauty.

Being global today is often a matter of exporting an ideology – taking a company brand or a company culture and inserting it into any or all markets around the world.

For the moment, there's money to be made along this route. But it's limited. It creates consistency, but leaves no room for surprise. It replicates a pattern, but doesn't create something new – it produces a series of units, all emotionally linked to a national home base, but it doesn't create a new, worldwide community.

Homogeneity, in the longer term, is no route to success. People are tired of sameness.

Exporting ideology, equally, won't guarantee success. Organizations that offer a little piece of America, say, or a little piece of England still have a glamour. But that won't last. McDonald's will no longer be good just because it's American, Burberry will no longer sell just because it's British. (Rover cars have found this out already.) People want something they can belong to, not just something foreign they can be impressed by (or impress their friends with).

So the new global organization will be different. It won't aim to create the same thing everywhere. It will become much more part of life wherever it is. It will be much more diverse. But uniting this diversity will be a big idea – not a national idea but a universal one.

The model could be a hotel group like Mandarin Oriental, which aims to create a family of very different hotels, each very much part of its home city, but sharing a universal idea about moments of pleasure.

On a much smaller scale, the National Trust has the universal big idea of 'places for people for ever', but its special skill is to find and protect, in each of those places, the intangible something that makes it unique – the something that the ancient world called the *genius loci*, the spirit of the place. No other conservation organization is as good as the National Trust at looking after the spirit of the place. There's an instructive paradox here: the National Trust's unifying idea is diversity. What its places have in common is the very fact that they have nothing in common.

What the National Trust knows, and what Mandarin Oriental knows, is that – contrary to the current business mantra – geography is not history. It never will be. Place will always matter. Place is what people belong to. Place is the thing that communities grow around. Place – the spirit of the place – is what gives the world its colour, its differences, its beauty.

For the moment, of course, the rise of standardization continues. Starbucks continues to open coffee shops in cities all over the world, offering much the same formula everywhere. And there is a role for this kind of consistency. People will want certain things to be consistent, to be the same everywhere. But the place to go for consistency will be the internet. That's where people will go for experiences that can be the same anywhere – indeed that *have* to be the same everywhere, because the internet is one of the very few creations of humankind that has no connection with place, that isn't in any sense *local*. The internet is where people will go for insurance, electricity, t-shirts, money, air tickets, pharmaceuticals.

But the neighbourhood shopping street is where people will go for *inconsistency*. For better coffee, unique bread, hand-made clothes, a doctor's reassurance, an artist's installation, a musician's performance. The shopping street will be home to smaller, more individual enterprises. These enterprises won't care about size. Their passion will be beauty. They will be a mosaic rather than a monolith: the place to go in an age of nonconformity.

From managing to inspiring

Once we start to think of organizations as communities, everything changes. Traditional roles start to become meaningless. The old distinctions between different stakeholders start to blur.

Employees get more like customers, because they choose whether or not to 'buy' the values of the community – and if they don't, they go elsewhere. The same is true for investors.

Meanwhile, customers start to look like employees, because they become contributors and participants, not just passive recipients of a product or service. And suppliers and distributors become much closer to the organization – not fighting it for the best deal, but contributing to its big idea.

The old words, as a result, no longer feel adequate.

An 'employee' is merely someone who's employed, but the role is now much more active than that.

Equally, the word 'consumer' is wrong: what matters isn't passive consumption but active contribution.

And no word is more inadequate than 'manager'. As organizations become communities, what's essential isn't managing people but inspiring them.

In the new marketplace, the most important kinds of managing are very different from what we've seen in the past. Thinking is becoming less important, feeling more.

Think about the paradoxical skills involved in finding a big idea. Searching, but also being open to chance discovery. Getting to know the organization's inside world – its character, its personality, its passions – but also sensing where the outside world is going. Most important of all, understanding the past, but also imagining the future.

Think too about the attitude and verve needed to cross the shadows that fall between conceiving the big idea and creating it out in the world.

And think of the sensitivity and self-awareness needed to keep the idea alive, through the seven ages: knowing by a kind of instinct whether the time is right to concentrate on the core of the big idea, or whether to open it out to new possibilities, whether to bring people closer together, or whether to encourage dissent.

It's all very different from that twentieth-century hope that management could be scientific. In many ways, the twentieth-century corporation was constructed to give science its best chance – to apply as much structure and uniformity and predictability as possible. But the twenty-first-century community is a very different place. People are challenging structure, fighting uniformity, enjoying surprise. The often dismal science of management has given way to the much more exciting art of inspiration.

Leap of faith

No longer is 'best practice' any kind of guide to the future. Until recently, organizations derived a great deal of reassurance from checking out their rivals, 'benchmarking' themselves against other companies, and finding what seemed to be the best ways of doing things. It was a sound, rational, scientific thing to do.

But in the new way of business, it's pointless. The best way to do things hasn't yet been invented. And more to the point, the best way for you to do things is *your way*, not someone else's. This poses a real challenge to management consultants who specialize in finding and spreading best practice. They'll need instead to help their clients look forwards, rather than looking over their shoulders, and to find creativity inside rather than outside. In the new way of business, invention is better than emulation. The real source of energy is being yourself. It's a frightening thought – it's much easier to follow what others have done.

The new way of business, to put this another way, is about uncharted territory – not about treading carefully in others' footsteps. And in uncharted territory, there's a better guide than rationality: intuition. Intuition is that remarkable faculty that interrogates our experience and enables us to *feel* what's the right thing to do, even in a situation we've never encountered before. Most of us are educated to blot out our intuition, and to make reasoned decisions based on ascertainable facts. But in the new way of business, the most interesting facts aren't ascertainable. There's no right answer. The right decision is often simply the one you're most committed to following through. The right thing to do is to follow your passions.

The organizations that succeed in the new way of business – the communities that thrive – will be those who don't do the rational thing. Those who don't emulate but invent. Those who don't analyse the 'critical success factors' but imagine what success would feel like. Those who trust their collective intuition. Those who are prepared to make a leap of faith. It's not a science – and the truth is, it never was.

It means jumping into space. It's like the Christopher Logue poem at 3i. Inspiring people means going beyond what you can rationally justify, moving outside the safe ground, saying with great confidence what you don't quite feel confident about.

This is not a blind irrationalism – it's not opposed to reason. It just knows that reason and calculation aren't always our best guides, and often distract us from what we know in our heart is the right thing to do.

This leap of faith is what the organizations I've been talking about did, and still do. Faith that a bank can be scrupulously fair, and yet still make money. Faith that computers can be almost human. Faith that an energy company can both provide fuel and protect the environment. Faith that customers are indeed smart. Faith that people want to be treated with respect rather than deference. Faith that good design really matters. Faith that you can make a better form of capitalism. Faith that you can create harmony between car companies, car workers and car owners. Faith that perfection is achievable. Faith that you can make better wine than the French. Faith that coffee could become a cult. Faith that a small iconoclastic company can take on the established giants.

No doubt there are many thousands more organizations with faith like this around the world – perhaps including yours. What they've all found is that by imagining how things could be different and better – how the world *ought* to be – they've helped make things different and better.

Rather than trying to research a future that doesn't yet exist, or second-guess the competition, they've followed their own instincts, and made their own future. And that future has become our future – not a narrow gain that belongs to a corporation but a wider achievement that belongs to us all.

CATALOGUE

the good idea guide

This is a catalogue of 50 of the biggest ideas around at the moment. It's not intended to be exhaustive, but it does include most of the organizations that I discuss in detail in the book. The big idea isn't always, or even usually, the organization's own words – it's my interpretation of what the organization's words and deeds add up to. The score – up to a maximum of five stars – is based on my judgement of how big an idea it is: how radical, how social and how tangible.

Organization	Idea	Activity	Verdict	Score
3i	The creative use of money	Provider of venture capital	A big idea that's still palpable in the organization.	☆☆☆
Amazon	Complete-ness	Internet retailer	A big idea, but not yet emotional enough.	☆☆☆
Apple	Usability	Computer maker	Idea that's kept Apple alive and influenced the whole personal computer industry.	☆☆☆☆☆
Aveda	Purity	Cosmetics maker	An idea simple enough to create a very distinctive experience for customers.	☆☆☆☆

Organization	Idea	Activity	Verdict	Score
Bang & Olufsen	Poetry	Hi-fi maker	A bigger way of thinking about technology that's given Bang & Olufsen a unique longevity.	☆☆☆☆
BBC	Authoritative	Broadcaster	A huge idea, more strongly felt outside than inside Britain.	☆☆☆
Ben & Jerry's	Home-made	Ice-cream maker	An idea that caught one aspect of the public mood.	☆☆☆☆
Benetton	Humanity	Clothing maker and retailer	Impressive idea, but delivered more through adverts than products.	☆☆
Body Shop	Green	Cosmetics retailer	Still a big idea, but others have caught up.	☆☆☆
BP	Beyond Petroleum	Energy producer and distributor	High-profile and high-risk new idea, challenging the conventions of the oil industry.	☆☆☆☆
Channel 4	Difference	Broadcaster	Has successfully refocused in a world that had caught up.	☆☆☆☆
Charles Schwab	Customers are smart	Discount stockbroker	Deeply refreshing idea in world of financial services.	☆☆☆

Organization	Idea	Activity	Verdict	Score
Cisco	Outside in	Network equipment maker	An idea of the moment, fuelling one of the world's new giants.	☆☆☆
Coca-Cola	Real thing	Soft drinks maker	An idea that makes Coca-Cola hard to topple as brand leader.	☆☆
Dell	Direct	Computer maker	A business model that's grown into a big idea.	☆☆☆
Disney	Fun	Media giant	Hard to imagine a simpler, more resonant idea.	☆☆☆☆
Fannie Mae	Home-ownership	Mortgage funds provider	Tightly specified idea has fuelled fast growth.	☆☆☆☆
First Direct	Banking to suit the customer	Phone and internet banker	Worked brilliantly for ten years, but what's next?	☆☆☆☆
Gap	Democratic fashion	Clothing retailer	Plenty of mileage in this still.	☆☆☆☆
General Electric	Learning	Industrial, media and financial giant	Big internally, not so relevant to customers.	☆☆
Go	Equality	Low-cost airline	Absolutely right for the current mood.	☆☆☆☆

Organization	Idea	Activity	Verdict	Score
The Guardian	Outsider	Newspaper and internet publisher	Will be hugely relevant in new multi-channel world.	☆☆☆☆
Heathrow Express	Seamless travel	Airport railway operator	Great idea; the challenge is to keep delivering it.	☆☆☆☆
Herman Miller	Good design	Office furniture maker	Has differentiated Herman Miller for over 50 years.	☆☆☆☆
Hewlett-Packard	Invent	Computer equipment maker	Very promising rediscovery of founding impulse.	☆☆
HSBC	One bank for the world	Banker	Could be big, but early days yet; a bit dry.	☆☆
IKEA	Democrat-izing design	Furnishings retailer	Wonderful idea with huge potential for new activities.	☆☆☆☆☆
John Lewis Partnership	A better form of capitalism	Retailer	Still unique and much loved idea in British retailing.	☆☆☆☆☆
The Landmark Trust	Mildly elevating experiences	Restorer of old build-ings as holiday lets	Unusual and intriguing, though a little high-minded.	☆☆☆☆
Mandarin Oriental	Moments of pleasure	Hotel company	Much more sophisticated idea than most hotel chains.	☆☆☆☆

Organization	Idea	Activity	Verdict	Score
Marks & Spencer	Respect-ability	Retailer	Idea needs to be updated – the new respectability.	☆☆
McKinsey	Rigour	Manage-ment consultants	Needs reorienting for the less rationalistic new century.	☆☆☆☆
Microsoft	Ubiquity	Software maker	More about vaulting ambition than emotional resonance.	☆☆
Muji	No brand	Clothing and house-wares retailer	Plainness is still hugely attractive in a garish marketplace.	☆☆☆☆
The National Trust	Places for people for ever	Conser-vation charity	Means more to people now than ever.	☆☆☆☆
Nike	Winning	Sports shoe maker	Could lose its appeal in a less competitive new century.	☆☆☆
Nokia	Future-leaning	Maker of mobile phones and related software	Powerful idea with strong Finnish flavour that has helped make Nokia pre-eminent.	☆☆☆☆
Orange	Optimism	Mobile phone operator	How will Orange modulate the idea for the internet age?	☆☆☆☆

Organization	Idea	Activity	Verdict	Score
Pret a Manger	Passion	Sandwich shop operator	An idea that's transformed the whole business of lunch.	☆☆☆☆
Saturn	Harmony	Car maker	Certainly resonates – but do the products deliver it?	☆☆☆☆
Shell	Stakeholder in society	Energy producer and distributor	An idea felt more strongly inside than outside Shell.	☆☆
Shiseido	Thankfulness	Cosmetics maker	There's no other idea remotely like it.	☆☆☆
The Soil Association	Organics	Campaign-ing charity	An idea that's 50 years old but whose time has finally come.	☆☆☆☆
Sony	Miniature perfection	Maker of consumer electronics	Fascinating because unachievable idea.	☆☆☆☆
Southcorp	World wine	Wine maker	An idea that's transformed wine making and drinking worldwide.	☆☆☆☆
Southwest Airlines	Irreverence	Low-cost airline	Has given Southwest a position no one else can grab.	☆☆☆☆

Organization	Idea	Activity	Verdict	Score
Starbucks	Coffee as cult	Coffee shop operator	An idea so seductive, people are starting to worry Starbucks is too powerful.	☆☆☆☆
Tesco	We like our customers	Retailer	An idea that's been delivered in many different ways in Tesco's 80-year history.	☆☆☆☆
Virgin	Iconoclasm	Financial services company, airline, retailer, and so on	A youthful idea that continues to be irresistible to an ageing population.	☆☆☆☆☆
Wal-Mart	Folksy value	Retailer	All-conquering – so far.	☆☆☆

notes

competence', *Harvard Business Review*, January–February 2000, p. 81.

48 'We, the individuals, aren't ownable any more . . .': Charles Handy, *The Hungry Spirit* (Hutchinson, London, 1997), p. 8.

48 'Businesses that fail to engage . . .': Thomas Petzinger, *The New Pioneers* (Simon & Schuster, New York, 1999), p. 25.

51 'Thanks largely to the Internet . . .': C. K. Prahalad and Venkatram Ramaswamy, 'Co-opting customer competence', p. 80.

4. Towards a big idea

58 'Stick to the knitting': Tom Peters and Robert H. Waterman, *In Search of Excellence* (HarperCollins, London, 1995).

59 'The existence of a core ideology . . .': James C. Collins and Jerry I. Porras, *Built to Last* (Century, London, 1998), p. 54.

63 'A talisman, hung in public places . . .': Eileen C. Shapiro, *Fad Surfing in the Boardroom* (Capstone, Oxford, 1996), p. 15.

68 'The unity of feeling which pervaded . . .': *The Economist*, 13 February 1999.

72 'There is one thing stronger . . .': *The Nation*, 15 April 1943.

5. The soul of the organization

75 'One of those concepts that . . .': Charles Handy, *The Hungry Spirit*, p. 158.

75 'Cannot commit treason . . .': Anthony Sampson, *Company Man* (HarperCollins, London, 1995), p. 17.

76 'Definition is the enclosing . . .': Samuel Butler, *Notebooks* (A. C. Fifield, London, 1912), ch. 14.

78 'Our model is work hard . . .': *Observer*, 24 January 1999.

78 'I may be a businessman . . .' Richard Branson, *Losing my Virginity* (Virgin Publishing, London, 1998), p. 480.

78 'So hard that if you don't have a passion . . .': *Fortune*, 24 January 2000.

80 'In combining social progress . . .': James Walvin, *The Quakers: Money and Morals* (John Murray, London, 1997), p. 185.

82 'Solves the functional problem . . .': *Fast Company*, November 1999.

85 'We sell fun . . .': 'Common sense and conflict: an interview with Disney's Michael Eisner', *Harvard Business Review*, January–February 2000, p. 122.

85 'Most of the time . . .': www.ikea.com, 1999.

92 'Have you ever heard of . . .': *Independent*, 26 January 2000.

92 'Bringing business to

minorities . . .': *Fortune*, 3 August 1999.

93 'We have more to do . . .': *Fortune*, 3 August 1999.

6. Starting the journey

98 'Starbucks changed coffee drinking . . .': W. Chan Kim and Renee Mauborgne, *Financial Times*, 20 May 1999.

98 'More than any other element . . .': Richard Branson, *Losing my Virginity*, p. 475.

100 'Policy is about political will . . .' Bob Garratt, *The Fish Rots From the Head* (HarperCollins, London 1996), p. 44.

103 'It's more fun to be a pirate . . .': Anthony Sampson, *Company Man*, p. 191.

105 'The customer is a rear-view mirror': Tom Peters, *The Circle of Innovation*, p. 326.

105 'This is what customers pay us for . . .': *Fortune*, 24 January 2000.

105 'My staff are maddened . . .': Richard Branson, *Losing my Virginity*, p. 488.

105 'To peel back the layers of a customer . . .': *Fast Company*, February 1999.

106 'We've reached the limits . . .': Gary Hamel and C. K. Prahalad, *Competing for the Future* (Harvard Business School Press,

Cambridge, MA, 1996), p. x.

108 'History can't be left . . .': Max De Pree, *Leadership Jazz* (Dell, New York, 1992), p. 75.

108 'Finns do not make a big noise . . .': *Financial Times*, 24 March 1999.

110 'I just bought what I liked . . .': Tom Peters, *The Circle of Innovation*, p. 326.

7. Crossing the shadows

120 'In just a few more years . . .': Rick Levine, Christopher Locke, Doc Searls and David Weinberger, *The Cluetrain Manifesto* (Perseus, Cambridge, MA, 2000), p. xiii.

126 'There's something new and daring . . .': Michael Maccoby, 'Narcissistic Leaders', *Harvard Business Review*, January–February 2000, p. 69.

127 'AA staff now see themselves . . .': Kevin Thomson, *Emotional Capital* (Capstone, Oxford, 1998), p. 28.

132 'The company watches . . .': 'Common sense and conflict: an interview with Disney's Michael Eisner', p. 121.

133 'Who we are as people . . .': 'Common sense and conflict: an interview with Disney's Michael Eisner', p. 121.

134 'It's like a synergy boot

camp . . .': 'Common sense and conflict: an interview with Disney's Michael Eisner', p. 120.

138 'At some companies . . .': Max De Pree, *Leadership Jazz*, p. 71.

8. The seven ages of a big idea

146 'We think a company . . .': www.saturn.com, 2000.

149 'We're trying to use . . .': *Fortune*, 24 January 2000.

152 'Beyond Petroleum . . .': *Financial Times* 19 April 2001.

9. All the difference

163 'John Lewis achieves a profit . . .': *Evening Standard*, 17 September 1999.

165 'They can be compelling . . .': Michael De Kare-Silver, *Strategy in Crisis* (Macmillan, London, 1997), p. 185.

166 'Orange's revenue per user': figures from Orange.

168 'Urge others to join the club': Tom Peters, *The Circle of Innovation*, p. 459.

170 'Working here is a truly unbelievable experience': *Fortune*, 12 January 1998.

176 'In 1988, for example . . .': report by Citibank and Interbrand Newell and Sorrell, 1999.

176 'Financial metrics are lagging indicators . . .': *Measures that Matter*, Ernst & Young survey, 1998, p. 2.

182 'If you don't stand for something . . .': www.reebok.com, 1999.

184 'Charles Handy talks . . .': a private presentation, 1999.

10. New business

197 'The balanced scorecard': see Robert S. Kaplan and David P. Norton, *The Balanced Scorecard* (Harvard Business School Press, Cambridge, MA, 1996). Kaplan explains: 'The Balanced Scorecard retains financial measures, such as return-on-capital-employed and economic value added, and supplements these with new measures on value creation for customers, enhancement of internal processes, including innovation, to deliver desired value propositions to targeted customers, and the creation of capabilities in employees and systems.'

further reading

These are the books that have most effectively informed, inspired or provoked me.

Aaker, David A., *Building Strong Brands* (Free Press, New York, 1996)

Branson, Richard, *Losing my Virginity* (Virgin Publishing, London, 1998)

Collins, James C. and Jerry I. Porras, *Built to Last* (Century, London, 1998)

de Gues, Arie, *The Living Company* (Nicholas Brearley, London, 1997)

de Kare-Silver, Michael, *Strategy in Crisis* (Macmillan, London, 1997)

De Pree, Max, *Leadership Jazz* (Dell, New York, 1992)

Evans, Philip and Thomas S. Wurster, *Blown to Bits* (Harvard Business School Press, Cambridge, MA, 1999)

Garratt, Bob, *The Fish Rots From the Head* (HarperCollins, London, 1996)

Gates, Bill, *The Road Ahead* (Viking Penguin, New York, 1995)

Hamel, Gary and C. K. Prahalad, *Competing for the Future* (Harvard Business School Press, Cambridge, MA, 1996)

Handy, Charles, *The Hungry Spirit* (Hutchinson, London, 1997)

Jensen, Rolf, *The Dream Society* (McGraw-Hill, New York, 1999)

Jones, Stokes, editor, *Issues Book: Planning for Social Change 1999* (Henley Centre, London, 1999)

Klein, Naomi, *No Logo* (Flamingo, London, 2000)

Levine, Rick, Christopher Locke, Doc Searls and David Weinberger, *The Cluetrain Manifesto* (Perseus, Cambridge, MA, 2000)

Levy, Steven, *Insanely Great* (Penguin, London, 1995)

Ormerod, Paul, *Butterfly Economics* (Faber, London, 1998)

Peters, Tom, *The Circle of Innovation* (Alfred A. Knopf, New York, 1997)

Pine II, Joseph P. and James H. Gilmore, *The Experience Economy* (Harvard Business School Press, Cambridge, MA, 1999)

Popcorn, Faith, *Clicking* (HarperCollins, London, 1996)

Sampson, Anthony, *Company Man* (HarperCollins, London, 1995)

Thomson, Kevin, *Emotional Capital* (Capstone, Oxford, 1998)

Walvin, James, *The Quakers: Money and Morals* (John Murray, London, 1997)

Winsemius, Pieter, *The Emotional Revolution* (McKinsey & Company, Amsterdam, 1999)

index